Wanda E. Brunstetter's

Amish Friends

Healthy Options

Cookbook

BARBOUR
PUBLISHING

Published by Barbour Publishing, Inc., 1810 Barbour Drive, Uhrichsville, OH 44683, www.barbourbooks.com

Our mission is to inspire the world with the life-changing message of the Bible.

Member of the
Evangelical Christian
Publishers Association

Printed in China.

TABLE of CONTENTS

INTRODUCTION

When my children were still in school, I began having some health issues. After seeing several doctors and having numerous tests run, no one could find an answer for why I was losing weight and experiencing a multitude of symptoms, including sinus troubles that would not go away. It wasn't until I began seeing a naturopathic doctor and changed my way of eating, as well as taking some helpful supplements, that I was able to get better. Needless to say, the food I ate and served to my family quickly changed and has been a part of my life ever since.

Although many of the recipes that have been given to me over the years from friends and relatives are not conducive to my current diet, I have enjoyed altering them to be gluten-free and sugar-free, so they are healthier for me. Some of those recipes I have shared in this cookbook.

Many of my Amish friends choose to cook healthy meals too, and much of it is grown in their own gardens. My husband Richard and I recently ate at an Amish friend's home, where we enjoyed fresh tomatoes, corn on the cob, tasty cucumbers, and several other items of produce from their bountiful garden. It's a pleasure for me to cook meals with vegetables and fruits from my own garden.

Richard and I have enjoyed many wonderful meals served to us in Amish friends' homes. I most often return to our house with healthy recipes and healthy option tips our dear friends have graciously shared, such as those found in this book. I hope you will enjoy the nutritious recipes and suggestions included in the cookbook that are made with healthy ingredients and served in Amish homes and for various functions Amish and other Plain people often attend.

A special thank-you goes to my editor, Rebecca Germany, for compiling a good many of the recipes that were submitted by Amish friends.

—WANDA E. BRUNSTETTER

He makes grass grow for the cattle, and plants for people to cultivate—bringing forth food from the earth.
PSALM 104:14

HOW TO USE THIS COOKBOOK

All the diets work and none of them work.

–GIN STEPHENS, *Delay, Don't Deny: Living an Intermittent Fasting Lifestyle*

The body is a wonderful thing designed by our awesome Creator. No two people are alike. We are made up of a multitude of cells and genes that create very unique individuals. How our ancestors lived is part of our genes, and how and where we live today affects every aspect of our lives.

For someone to say that we all should eat one certain way just isn't right. We can't insist that everyone eat grains every day when a growing number of humans are experiencing gluten sensitivity. Likewise, some people thrive on good-quality dairy products while milk upsets others' digestive systems. Some people feel great eating a diet rich in healthy carbs while others do best on a low-carb diet.

We would do well to listen to our own bodies and determine what foods help us function optimally. Therefore, this cookbook won't tell you one way to eat. Amish and Mennonite cooks have shared the recipes that work for their families. The editing team has noted recipes that fit under certain labels that are important in today's health culture–dairy-free, gluten-free, sugar-free, low-carb, and so on. Look for recipes you are interested in by their category, such as main dishes, desserts, or snacks, and then note below the recipe names the health labels we've determined they fit under. Please excuse any mistakes made, for we are not food scientists.

We have also included a section of home remedies. Please don't take anything you read here as replacement for your doctor's advice or emergency medical attention. All home remedies should only be tried with a healthy dose of common sense and caution.

We hope you find some good recipes and tips here to help you and your family thrive.

—REBECCA GERMANY, editor

Is anyone among you sick? Let them call the elders of the church to pray over them and anoint them with oil in the name of the Lord. And the prayer offered in faith will make the sick person well; the Lord will raise them up. If they have sinned, they will be forgiven.

JAMES 5:14–15

SUPERFOODS

Greetings from Belize.

I enjoy reading and learning about health foods and more since I must watch my sugar intake. I like to make and raise as much of our food as possible. We produce eggs, cheese, butter, milk, and meat on the farm plus lots of different types of roots like potatoes and yams. I've switched to using cassava flour and arrowroot in my baking, and we are blessed to be able to grow our own cassava root and arrowroot here in Belize.

See my recipe for pancake mix using cassava flour on page 52 and arrowroot crackers on page 146.

MRS. WOLLIE (MARY) MILLER, Belize

Here are several benefits of daily consumption of fresh fruits and vegetables that I've discovered:

- Help prevent cancer
- Fight cancer cells in those already infected
- Help prevent diabetes
- Lower or regulate blood sugar
- Lower bad cholesterol
- Prevent strokes
- Lower risk of heart disease
- Strengthen the heart
- Improve memory and clarity
- Promote healthy kidneys, liver, and other organs
- Build up the immune system
- Strengthen bones, teeth, and nails
- Build healthy cells and repair unhealthy ones
- Provide healthy, glowing skin
- Strengthen hair and give it a healthy shine
- Improve eyesight
- Fight cataracts and blindness
- Keep digestive system healthy and working smoothly

- Provide fiber, which cleans the gut and slows the absorption of sugar
- Build up red blood cells
- Prevent anemia
- Slow the effects of aging
- Prevent or treat arthritis and rheumatism
- Fight damage to our bodies caused by contact with pollution, radiation, etc.
- Prevent or reduce inflammation in the body, the main cause of obesity, heart disease, cancer, and many other problems
- Help prevent weight gain
- Increase energy

Some of my favorite superfoods:

Avocado[1]

Avocados have been called "the world's healthiest food" for good reasons. They are packed with nutrients that build up our bodies and help protect us from several major health problems. Avocados have been shown to fight cancer cells in cancer patients while building up the healthy cells. They have also been shown to help prevent heart disease as well as protect against arthritis by reducing inflammation in the joints.

The calories in avocados are mostly from fat, but this is good, necessary fat that our bodies use to build healthy cells. This fat is burned slowly by the body as energy and makes us feel full longer. Health experts have recommended that we eat at least one avocado a day. The most nutrient-rich part of the avocado is the darkest part right next to the skin, so try not to miss out on it.

Beauty tip: The fat in avocados is also very good for your skin and fights wrinkling caused by overexposure to harsh sunlight. If you rub the dark green part against your skin, you will have one of the best face masks. Rinse your face with cold water and pat dry. Spread the avocado all over your face and leave for up to 30 minutes until dry. Wash off with warm water and pat face dry. Do as often as you like. You should soon notice that your skin looks healthier and feels firmer.

---

1   Kris Gunnars, "12 Proven Health Benefits of Avocado," *Healthline*, June 29, 2018, https://www.healthline.com/nutrition/12-proven-benefits-of-avocado#7.

Beans

Eating at least three cups of cooked beans each week is recommended, and more is fine. They are a good source of protein, which means that if we can't afford meat often, beans can take its place. No need to be embarrassed that beans are sometimes called "the poor man's meat." They are high in fiber, which helps keep you feeling full longer. Fiber helps to lower cholesterol and regulate blood sugar. Beans are also high in magnesium, so they might help with migraines. But the most important benefit of beans is that they actually lower the risk of breast cancer. Isn't that nice to know?

Cooking tip: Cook beans in unsalted chicken or beef broth to add even more nutrition and flavor to this heart-healthy food.

Callaloo (Amaranth)

That scraggly looking weed in your yard called callaloo or amaranth is actually very good for you. This is one weed you should allow to grow in your yard or garden. It is good for the heart for it helps regulate blood pressure and may even prevent cancer. Because it has a lot of protein and carbohydrates, callaloo will also give you energy. And, as a dark green, leafy vegetable, it contains iron, which builds up red blood cells and helps protect from anemia.

Harvest the leaves when they are fairly young. You can eat the stems too, but you might have to peel them. The plant should grow back even as the top leaves are harvested. Add callaloo to soups, scrambled eggs, salad, or whatever you prefer.

Interesting facts: There are many different varieties of amaranth worldwide. Most people also eat the seeds. They can be eaten by those who are allergic to wheat and other grains. The seeds are cooked like oatmeal for cereal or like rice. They can even be popped like popcorn or ground into flour.

Citrus Fruits

Citrus fruits like oranges, limes, lemons, and grapefruit provide almost every single benefit I listed under the benefits of consuming fruits and vegetables.

Oranges are a far better snack choice for your children than chips or biscuits (cookies).

Lime juice is very good for you, but we tend to add a lot of sugar to make it pleasant to drink. The healthiest way to enjoy lime juice is to squeeze a fresh lime into a glass of water and drink it straight with no sugar. (Though a little honey or stevia could be added.)

Lemon or lime juice is good for detoxing and can help dissolve kidney stones. The juice is also very soothing and cooling for a feverish person to drink.

Don't forget grapefruit. It may not be the most pleasant-tasting fruit, but that shouldn't stop you from finding ways to include it in your diet.

Cooking tip: Spice up your food by squeezing fresh lime juice on it. Add it to salad dressings and fruit juice mixes.

Beauty tip: Lime juice is good to use as a face wash to get rid of pimples. Dilute it in a bit of water before applying to skin.

Pineapple[2]

Who doesn't like this sweet, juicy treat? Pineapples are best eaten fresh to get all the benefits.

If you are down with a cold and cough, slice up a pineapple and eat as much as you want. Pineapple contains bromelain, which will help loosen mucous and let you cough it out. Pineapple can also help ease the pain of arthritis while strengthening bones. It helps relieve nausea and is a good snack if you are dealing with morning sickness. And it is a delicious way to fight intestinal worms.

Sweet Potatoes

Sweet potatoes are one root vegetable you want to be sure to include in your diet on a weekly basis if possible. Sweet potatoes are far better for you than regular white potatoes, cassava, or melanga coco root, and they are most nutritious when steamed or boiled just until soft enough to eat. Don't overcook. They offer protection from cancer and heart disease and are good for skin, hair, and eyes.

Ginger[3]

Excellent as a remedy for digestive problems and gas, ginger has been shown

---

2   "Other Home Remedies," MedicalNewsToday, accessed October 20, 2020, https://www.medicalnewstoday.com/articles/319126#other-home-remedies-for-coughs.

3   Densak Pongrajpaw, Charinthip Somprasit, Athita Chanthasenanont, "A Randomized Comparison of Ginger and Dimenhydrinate in the Treatment of Nausea and Vomiting in Pregnancy," PubMed.gov, September 2007, https://pubmed.ncbi.nlm.nih.gov/17957907/; Anahad O'Connor, "The Claim: Eating Ginger Can Cure Motion Sickness," *New York Times*, August 21, 2007, https://www.nytimes.com/2007/08/21/health/21real.html.

in a Danish study to be effective in relieving the symptoms of rheumatoid arthritis if given at the rate of just less than a tablespoon per day. Another study showed ginger powder in capsules to be more effective than Dramamine for preventing motion sickness. Ginger is also one of our best sources of zinc. So many benefits the Creator concentrated into one spicy, flavorful root!

Ginger is used traditionally in both savory and sweet dishes. Powdered ginger is an ingredient in curry powder. Fresh ginger can be finely shredded to season chicken or other meats, along with onions, garlic, and annatto (this tropical seed can be replaced with paprika and turmeric). In Asian cuisine, fresh ginger is a common ingredient in stir-fried vegetables. On the sweet side, ginger goes with cinnamon, allspice, nutmeg, and cloves to flavor apple or pumpkin pies and cakes.

Did your mother give you ginger ale when you were sick? If so, she was—perhaps unknowingly—following the traditional knowledge of ginger's healing properties, especially for upset stomach. Modern ginger ale and other such drinks, though, are carbonated by mechanical means, adding carbon dioxide to create a fizzy effect and bypassing the lacto-fermentation that gives ginger ale the most benefits. Humans have traditionally enjoyed these naturally fizzy and somewhat sweet drinks that are essential to intestinal health. The same cannot be said of modern sugar-laden soda pop beverages. (See my recipe for Lacto-Fermented Ginger Ale on page 14.)

God is our refuge and strength,
an ever-present help in trouble.

PSALM 46:1

BEVERAGES

"Worship the LORD your God, and his blessing
will be on your food and water. I will take
away sickness from among you."

EXODUS 23:25

> *"Coffee, even the decaffeinated version, appears to protect against type 2 diabetes. In a 2009 review, each additional daily cup of coffee lowered the risk of diabetes by 7 percent, even up to six cups per day."*
>
> —Dr. Jason Fung,
> *The Obesity Code: Unlocking the Secrets of Weight Loss*

Lacto-Fermented Ginger Ale

 DAIRY-FREE 🌾 GLUTEN-FREE 🥄 VEGAN

1 teaspoon ginger powder
8 cups water

1 cup sugar
Juice of 2 limes or lemons

Mix all ingredients together until sugar dissolves. You can drink it fresh, but fermented ginger ale has great intestinal benefits.

To ferment, pour ginger ale into glass bottles with screw-top lids. Cap and store at room temperature for several days. As it ages, it becomes stronger and less sweet. A little ginger ale from a previous batch added to a new batch will speed up fermentation from 3 days to 1 day. Keep old, too strong ginger ale for starter.

When you open a bottle of this ginger ale, it should hiss and fizz nicely like soda pop. However, on occasion, bottled ginger ale will spout out and make a mess. The remainder is still good to drink.

Mrs. Wollie (Mary) Miller, Belize

Beet Kvass

3 medium or 2 large organic beets, peeled and chopped
¼ cup whey

1 tablespoon sea salt
Filtered water

Place beets, whey, and salt in 2-quart glass container. Add filtered water to fill container. Stir well. Cover with towel. Keep at room temperature for 2 days. Strain and refrigerate. Add more water to beets and let sit at room temperature for 2 days. Results will be weaker than first batch. Discard beets after second batch.

Beet kvass is a valuable drink for its medicinal qualities. Beets are loaded with nutrients. One 4-ounce glass morning and night is an excellent blood tonic, promoter of regularity, digestive aid, blood alkalizer, liver cleanser, and treatment for kidney stones and other ailments. Beet kvass may also be used in place of vinegar in salads or as an addition to soups.

JERRY AND MARY GIROD, Carlisle, Kentucky

KOMBUCHA

3 quarts water
1 cup sugar
4 tea bags organic black tea

½ cup plain kombucha
1 kombucha mushroom

Bring water to boil. Add sugar, stirring to dissolve. Add tea bags and steep until water is cooled. Remove tea bags. Pour into gallon jar. Add kombucha and mushroom. Always stir with wooden spoon. Cover with clean cloth secured with rubber band. Put in warm, dark place. Let set 7 to 10 days or until kombucha suits your taste.

To flavor, set aside mushroom and at least ½ cup kombucha for next batch. Put kombucha in quart jars with ⅔ cup juice (e.g., blackberry, raspberry, grape, strawberry). Let set at room temperature for 1 to 2 days. Chill.

I usually make a new batch right away so that the mushroom is in use all the time.

BECKY FISHER, Lancaster, Pennsylvania

Healthy Cappuccino

GLUTEN-FREE SUGAR-FREE

1 teaspoon Dandy Blend
   drink mix
½ teaspoon carob powder
⅛ teaspoon stevia
Sprinkle cinnamon

Sprinkle nutmeg
¾ cup boiling water
¼ cup fresh goat milk
¼ teaspoon vanilla

In mug, combine Dandy Blend, carob powder, stevia, cinnamon, and nutmeg. Pour boiling water into cup and stir. Add milk and vanilla. Stir and enjoy.

Vera Mast, Kalona, Iowa

Iced Mocha Latte

DAIRY-FREE GLUTEN-FREE SUGAR-FREE VEGAN

5 to 6 cups hot strongly
   brewed coffee
2 tablespoons coconut oil
2 teaspoons stevia
¼ cup cocoa powder
1 tablespoon vanilla

1 teaspoon caramel extract
⅛ to ½ teaspoon cinnamon
Dash salt
14 drops English Toffee–
   flavored liquid stevia
1 cup almond milk

Combine all ingredients well in blender. To serve, pour over glassful of ice. Serve with a straw.

Vera Mast, Kalona, Iowa

Mocha Mix

4 cups instant nonfat dry
  milk
2 cups xylitol or Splenda

1 cup cocoa powder
½ teaspoon salt

Mix and store in airtight container.

For hot chocolate:
Use ¼ cup mix per cup of boiling water.

For mocha:
Use ¼ cup mix per cup of hot coffee and top with whipped cream.

Mrs. Albert (Ruth) Yoder, Stanwood, Michigan

Skinny Vanilla Iced Coffee

2 tablespoons Truvia
  sweetener
1 cup water
1 tablespoon vanilla
8 ounces strong brewed
  coffee, room temperature
  or chilled

½ cup ice
½ cup vanilla almond milk

To make simple syrup, combine Truvia and water in medium saucepan over medium heat. Stir in vanilla. Set aside to cool. Pour coffee over ice. Mix in almond milk. Stir in simple syrup to taste.

Katie Miller, Arthur, Illinois

Pumpkin Spice Latte

DAIRY-FREE | GLUTEN-FREE | REFINED–SUGAR FREE | VEGAN

1½ tablespoons pumpkin puree
2 tablespoons maple syrup
1 teaspoon pumpkin pie spice

8 ounces coffee
½ cup milk of choice
Cinnamon

Blend all ingredients except cinnamon in blender until smooth and creamy. Adjust seasonings as needed. Pour into mug and garnish with cinnamon. Serve immediately.

Loretta Brubaker, Farmington, Missouri

Berry Detox Smoothie

4 to 5 frozen strawberries

1 cup frozen blueberries

1 cup unsweetened almond
or coconut milk

1 tablespoon honey

1 tablespoon fresh
grated ginger

Juice from ½ lemon or
½ orange

Large handful baby spinach
or baby kale (optional)

1 tablespoon chia seed

Place strawberries, blueberries, milk, honey, ginger, juice, and spinach in blender. Blend until smooth. Stir in chia seeds.

Katie Miller, Arthur, Illinois

Energizing Carrot-Apple-Ginger Juice

11 small to medium organic carrots
4 organic Fuji apples, cored and sliced
1 thumb-sized piece organic ginger, peeled

Wash carrots and apples well. Press carrots, apples, and ginger through juicer. Mix well and serve immediately.

KATIE MILLER, Arthur, Illinois

Cranberry Cleanser Smoothie

1 large handful fresh baby
  kale or spinach
1 cup water

1 cup frozen cranberries
2 oranges
2 bananas

In blender, blend kale in water until broken down. Add cranberries, oranges, and bananas. Blend until smooth. Yields 2 servings.

EMMA MILLER, Baltic, Ohio

Cucumber Shake

2 cups chopped cucumbers
2 tablespoons instant nonfat
  dry milk
2 egg whites

Pinch salt
1 tablespoon lemon juice
1½ cups plain yogurt
3 ice cubes, cracked

Combine all ingredients in blender until smooth and frothy. Pour into chilled glasses and garnish with snipped parsley and chives if desired.

DAVID C. P. SCHWARTZ, Galesburg, Kansas

CAFÉ MOCHA SMOOTHIE

1 cup strong brewed
  coffee, cold
½ cup plain nonfat
  Greek yogurt
1 fresh or frozen
  banana, chunked

1 tablespoon unsweetened
  cocoa powder
Honey, to taste (optional)
Ice (optional)

Combine coffee, yogurt, banana, and cocoa in blender. Blend on high until creamy and well mixed. Add honey to taste. Blend in ice for thicker texture.

TIPS:

Add ¼ avocado, 1 tablespoon chia seed, or 1 tablespoon ground flaxseed for a more filling smoothie and a dose of heart-healthy fats.

Add a handful of baby spinach to sneak some vegetables into your smoothie.

KATIE MILLER, Arthur, Illinois

CHOCOLATE-COVERED STRAWBERRY SMOOTHIE

1 scoop chocolate bone
  broth powder
1 cup almond or rice milk

½ cup frozen strawberries
3 ice cubes

Combine all ingredients in blender until smooth. Yields 1 serving.

EMMA MILLER, Baltic, Ohio

Daily Green Bomb

1½ cups frozen mango chunks
2 celery stalks, chunked
1 large cucumber, thickly sliced
1 banana, chunked and frozen
½ cup parsley

½ cup cilantro
3 cups coconut water
1 tablespoon lemon juice
1 tablespoon lime juice
Water
Ice

Blend all ingredients except water and ice in heavy-duty blender. Add water and ice to reach desired consistency. Blend more if needed. Divide into 4 glasses, or divide into 4 pint jars, close tightly, and store in refrigerator. Use within 3 days.

KATHRYN TROYER, Rutherford, Tennessee

Simple Smoothie

1 banana
2 cups frozen strawberries
¾ cup frozen blueberries
1 cup unsweetened apple juice

2 scoops unflavored collagen powder

Layer in blender in order: banana, strawberries, blueberries, apple juice, and collagen. Blend until smooth. Yields 4 cups.

MARY MILLER, Shipshewana, Indiana

Snickers Smoothie

DAIRY-FREE GLUTEN-FREE SUGAR-FREE

½ cup raw cashews
1 scoop egg white powder
¼ cup sweetener of choice
½ cup cashew or
  almond milk
2 tablespoons unsweetened
  cocoa powder
3 tablespoons unsweetened
  peanut butter

1 teaspoon caramel flavoring
¾ teaspoon sea salt
14 ice cubes
2 tablespoons sugar-free,
  dairy-free chocolate chips
  (e.g., Lily's) (optional)
2 tablespoons dairy-free
  whipped topping

Blend in high-powered blender cashews, egg white powder, sweetener, milk, cocoa, peanut butter, caramel flavoring, and salt until smooth. Add ice cubes and blend. Stir in chocolate chips. Top with whipped topping. Eat with spoon.

Crystal Ropp, Kalona, Iowa

Chocolate Milkshake

GLUTEN-FREE REFINED SUGAR–FREE

10 ice cubes
½ cup heavy whipping cream
½ cup milk

1 tablespoon cocoa powder
¼ cup maple syrup

Combine all ingredients in blender until smooth.

Julia Troyer, Fredericksburg, Ohio

BREADS

Then Jesus declared, "I am the bread of life. Whoever comes to me will never go hungry, and whoever believes in me will never be thirsty."

JOHN 6:35

> *"The food you eat can either be the safest
> and most powerful form of medicine,
> or the slowest form of poison."*
>
> —Dr. Ann Wigmore

100% Whole Spelt Bread

2½ cups milk
1½ tablespoons yeast
½ cup water at 112 degrees
1 teaspoon honey
⅓ cup olive oil
⅓ cup maple syrup

1 or 2 eggs, beaten
9 cups spelt flour
1 tablespoon lecithin
½ teaspoon vitamin C
   powder (optional)
1½ tablespoons salt

In large saucepan, scald milk and cool to lukewarm. In small bowl, dissolve yeast in 112-degree water and honey. Add olive oil, maple syrup, and egg to milk. Stir in bloomed yeast. Gradually stir in 4 cups flour. Let set for 20 minutes at room temperature.

Add lecithin, vitamin C powder, salt, and rest of flour, trying to stir without ripping grains. Knead well. Grease large bowl and let dough rise for 3 hours at 70 degrees. Punch dough down gently and let rise another 1½ hours.

Shape into loaves and let set for 15 minutes. Roll into 7x12-inch rectangles with rolling pin. Roll dough into loaf. Let rise 30 to 45 minutes. Bake at 375 to 400 degrees for 10 minutes, decrease temperature to 325 to 350 degrees and bake about 20 minutes more.

A good soft bread.

Mrs. Joseph Miller, Gallipolis, Ohio

100% Organic Whole Grain Bread

EGG-FREE · NUT-FREE · REFINED SUGAR-FREE

Step 1:

6 cups organic whole grain flour

½ cup organic dairy whey

1¾ cups water

¾ cup organic butter, lard, or coconut oil

Combine all ingredients. Cover tightly and allow to sit in warm place 8 to 24 hours.

Step 2:

¼ cup warm (100 degrees) water

¼ cup organic raw honey

1½ tablespoons instant yeast

The next day, mix in glass bowl warm water, honey, and yeast. Let sit until it is frothy.

Step 3:

1 tablespoon Himalayan pink salt or Real Salt

¾ teaspoon baking soda

Add salt and baking soda to rested flour mixture. Stir well. Add yeast mixture, working yeast throughout flour with your fingers, pulling and stretching to incorporate it into lump.

Step 4:

1½ cups organic whole wheat or oat flour

When lump beings to form, add flour ½ cup at a time while kneading dough on clean surface. A long kneading time of 10 to 15 minutes but leaving dough as sticky as possible will provide nicest end result—and will provide a good workout too! Cover and let rise in warm place for about 2 hours.

Step 5:

Punch down dough and form into 2 loaves. Cover again and allow to rise until doubled in volume.

Step 6:

Bake at 350 degrees for 35 to 40 minutes. Cool loaves completely before bagging.

A warm slice of this bread with homemade cottage cheese and apple butter is a delicious and nutritious treat.

ADA J. MAST, Kalona, Iowa

Brown Bread

DAIRY-FREE **EGG-FREE** **NUT-FREE** **REFINED SUGAR-FREE** **VEGAN**

4 tablespoons maple syrup	1 teaspoon salt
2 teaspoons flour	⅓ cup oil
¾ cup warm water	1 cup whole wheat flour
1 tablespoon yeast	Sapphire flour

Mix maple syrup, 2 teaspoons flour, warm water, and yeast. Let set until mixture starts to rise. Add salt, oil, and wheat flour. Add sapphire flour until dough is smooth. Knead every 15 minutes for 1 hour. Place dough in greased pan and let rise until doubled. Bake at 350 degrees for 25 minutes or until golden. Yields 1 loaf.

LINDA BURKHOLDER, Fresno, Ohio

SPELT BREAD

DAIRY-FREE · EGG-FREE · NUT-FREE · REFINED SUGAR–FREE

1 cup lukewarm water
1 tablespoon yeast
½ cup honey
½ teaspoon salt
1 tablespoon olive oil

2 teaspoons molasses
1 vitamin C capsule (use only contents)
2½ cups spelt flour

Mix water, yeast, and honey; let set until yeast rises. Add salt, oil, molasses, and vitamin C; mix well. Add flour. Dough will be sticky. Let rise. Knead down 2 or 3 times. Place dough in 2 small loaf pans. Let rise 1 hour. Bake at 350 degrees for 35 minutes.

MRS. ROSIE SCHWARTZ, Salem, Indiana

FAVORITE GLUTEN–FREE BREAD

GLUTEN-FREE · NUT-FREE

2 cups rice flour
1¾ cups tapioca starch
3½ teaspoons xanthan gum
1½ tablespoons yeast
4 eggs

¼ cup sugar
1 teaspoon salt
2 teaspoons vinegar
¼ cup oil, butter, or lard
1¾ cups warm water

Mix rice flour, tapioca starch, xanthan gum, and yeast; set aside. In large bowl, beat eggs, sugar, salt, vinegar, oil, and water warm enough to make full mixture lukewarm. Add flour mixture and stir well for 5 minutes. Place in 2 greased loaf pans. Smooth top of batter with wet spatula. Let rise until doubled. Bake at 375 degrees for 40 minutes.

MARYANN STAUFFER, Homer City, Pennsylvania

Golden Flax Bread

2 cups golden flaxseed meal
1 tablespoon baking powder
¾ teaspoon salt
2 tablespoons coconut oil, melted

2 whole eggs
4 egg whites
¾ cup water
Pinch stevia

Mix flaxseed meal, baking powder, and salt. Add coconut oil, eggs, egg whites, water, and stevia. Mix well. Pour into well-greased or parchment-lined loaf pan. Let set for 5 minutes. Bake at 350 degrees for 25 to 30 minutes.

ESTHER L. MILLER, Fredericktown, Ohio

Gluten-Free Bread

6 cups gluten-free flour mix*
5 teaspoons xanthan gum
3 teaspoons salt
3 teaspoons unflavored gelatin
6 teaspoons instant yeast
4 eggs

⅓ cup vegetable oil
⅓ cup honey
2 teaspoons vinegar
½ to ¾ cup peeled and grated raw potato
2½ cups warm water

In bowl, sift together flour, xanthan gum, salt, gelatin, and yeast. In stand mixer bowl, blend eggs, oil, honey, and vinegar. Add potato and beat. Add water and beat. Gradually add dry mixture. Beat on highest speed for 3½ minutes. Spoon into 2 or 3 greased loaf pans and let rise for 10 minutes. Bake at 350 degrees for 25 minutes. Cover with foil and bake another 40 minutes. Best eaten fresh.

*GLUTEN-FREE FLOUR MIX
2 cups rice flour
1 cup tapioca starch

1 teaspoon xanthan gum

Mix well.

THE DAN D. YODERS, Mercer, Missouri

Sorghum Flour Bread

1½ teaspoons yeast

2 teaspoons sugar

1 cup warm water

1½ cups sorghum flour blend
(see page 158)

2 teaspoons xanthan gum

1 teaspoon unflavored
gelatin

1 teaspoon baking powder

¾ teaspoon salt

¼ teaspoon soy lecithin
(optional)

2 tablespoons butter, melted

2 large eggs

½ teaspoon cider vinegar

Combine yeast and sugar with warm water; set aside 5 minutes. Combine flour, xanthan gum, gelatin, baking powder, salt, and soy lecithin in mixing bowl. Add melted butter, eggs, and vinegar. Beat dough with electric mixer on high (using regular beaters, not dough hook) for 2 minutes. Dough will be very soft and sticky. Transfer to 6 greased 3x5½-inch pans (I use small foil pans). Spread dough to edges with wet spatula. Cover and let rise in warm place 20 to 30 minutes. Bake at 350 degrees for 25 to 30 minutes or until tops are golden brown and firm. Cool 5 minutes and remove from pans. Bread rises in oven, but once you remove it from oven, it will fall in pan, but that is okay. This is delicious soft bread that freezes well. Because there are no additives, it molds quickly.

SUSIE E. KINSINGER, Fredericktown, Ohio

Gluten-Free Buttermilk Biscuits

1 cup cornstarch (I prefer
  potato based.)
2 tablespoons brown sugar
1 cup brown rice flour
1 teaspoon xanthan gum
4 teaspoons baking powder

½ teaspoon baking soda
1 teaspoon Real Salt
4 tablespoons butter
1 cup buttermilk
2 egg whites
Cooking spray

In medium mixing bowl, combine cornstarch, brown sugar, flour, xanthan gum, baking powder, baking soda, and salt with fork until thoroughly mixed. Add butter and work into mixture until it gets crumbly. Add buttermilk and egg whites and work with fork until just combined. Bake at 400 degrees for 15 to 18 minutes or until golden brown. Yields 10 to 12 biscuits.

Mattie Hochstetler, Keytesville, Missouri

Healthy Biscuits

1 cup whole wheat pastry
  flour
2 tablespoons soy flour
2 tablespoons SNO*E TOFU
  powder
¾ cup unbleached white flour
2 tablespoons barley flour

½ teaspoon salt
4 teaspoons baking powder
1 beaten egg
½ teaspoon cream of tartar
2 tablespoons lecithin
¾ cup water

Combine all ingredients and turn onto surface dusted with unbleached flour. Knead only enough to be able to handle. Flatten ball to ½-inch thickness and cut with biscuit cutter or glass. (I just drop them.) Bake on cookie sheet at 375 degrees for 15 to 20 minutes. May be served with country gravy.

Susie E. Kinsinger, Fredericktown, Ohio

Buns

1 rounded tablespoon yeast
1½ cups warm water
¼ cup honey or agave
¼ cup corn oil

¾ teaspoon salt
1 tablespoon lecithin
1 tablespoon xanthan gum
4 to 5 cups brown rice flour

In large bowl, dissolve yeast in warm water. Add honey, oil, salt, lecithin, and xanthan gum. Gradually stir in flour. Dough will be sticky. Let rise 1 hour. Divide into 6 buns and place on greased cookie sheet. Let rise 15 to 20 minutes. Bake at 375 degrees for 20 minutes.

KATIE MILLER, Arthur, Illinois

Cheesy Garlic Breadsticks

3 eggs
½ cup almond flour
⅓ slightly heaping cup
   ground flaxseed meal
1 tablespoon butter, melted
2 tablespoons grated
   Parmesan cheese

½ teaspoon garlic powder
1 teaspoon Italian seasoning
¾ teaspoon baking powder
½ teaspoon salt

Mix all ingredients well and spread in greased 9x13-inch pan.

TOPPING:

1 teaspoon garlic powder
2 teaspoons Italian
   seasoning
1 teaspoon oregano

¼ cup grated Parmesan
   cheese
1¼ cups shredded cheese of
   your choice

Combine all ingredients and spread over bread batter. Bake at 350 degrees for 13 minutes. Cut into sticks.

FREIDA FISHER, Sprakers, New York

Flaxseed Raisin Bread

1 cup raisins
1 cup boiling water
1 teaspoon baking soda
1 cup whole wheat flour
1 cup oatmeal
¾ cup flaxseed meal
⅓ cup sugar or honey

1 tablespoon cinnamon
1 cup milk
1 teaspoon vanilla
1 teaspoon baking powder
1 cup boiling water
1 teaspoon baking soda

Combine raisins, boiling water, and baking soda to soak until raisins soften. In separate bowl, mix flour, oatmeal, flaxseed meal, sugar, cinnamon, milk, vanilla, and baking powder. Fold in raisins. Batter will be very moist. Pour into greased and floured 9x5-inch loaf pan. Bake at 350 degrees for 55 to 75 minutes.

MARYANN STAUFFER, Homer City, Pennsylvania

PUMPKIN BREAD

DAIRY-FREE **GLUTEN-FREE** **REFINED SUGAR–FREE**

1 cup almond flour
¼ cup coconut flour
½ teaspoon sea salt
½ teaspoon baking soda
1 teaspoon cinnamon
½ teaspoon pumpkin pie
   spice

¾ cup pumpkin puree
¼ cup maple syrup
¼ cup coconut oil, melted
3 large eggs

Combine almond flour, coconut flour, sea salt, baking soda, cinnamon, and pumpkin pie spice. Set aside. In another bowl, mix pumpkin puree, maple syrup, coconut oil, and eggs. Add dry mixture to wet mixture. Pour into greased loaf pan. Bake at 350 degrees for 45 to 60 minutes.

ESTHER L. MILLER, Fredericktown, Ohio

ZUCCHINI NUT BREAD

DAIRY-FREE **LOW-CARB** **SUGAR-FREE**

1 scant cup Atkins baking
   mix
1 scant cup finely ground
   almond flour
1½ cups granular sugar
   substitute
2 teaspoons cinnamon
1 teaspoon salt

1 teaspoon baking soda
½ teaspoon baking powder
1 cup vegetable oil
4 eggs
1 medium zucchini, coarsely
   grated
1 teaspoon vanilla

In large bowl, whisk together baking mix, almond flour, sugar substitute, cinnamon, salt, baking soda, and baking powder. In medium bowl, mix oil, eggs, zucchini, and vanilla. Combine mixtures and stir well. Pour into greased 4x8-inch loaf pan. Bake at 350 degrees for 1 hour until golden brown. Cool on wire rack before cutting into bars.

Note: To use batter for muffins, reduce baking time to 30 minutes.

MRS. DAVID KURTZ, Smicksburg, Pennsylvania

Banana–Blueberry Muffins

DAIRY-FREE · **EGG-FREE** · **NUT-FREE** · **VEGAN** · **NO ADDED SUGAR**

4 or 5 ripe bananas
½ cup unsweetened applesauce
1 teaspoon vanilla
3 tablespoons coconut oil, melted
1⅓ cups flour
2 to 4 tablespoons flaxseed meal
1 teaspoon baking soda
1 teaspoon cinnamon
½ teaspoon salt
1 to 2 cups fresh or frozen blueberries

In medium bowl, mash bananas. Add applesauce, vanilla, and coconut oil. Add flour, flaxseed meal, baking soda, cinnamon, and salt. Mix well and add blueberries. Grease or line muffin tins. Fill cups ¾ full. Bake at 350 degrees for 18 to 20 minutes.

EMMA BYLER, New Wilmington, Pennsylvania

Blueberry Muffins

GLUTEN-FREE · **NUT-FREE**

1 cup gluten-free quick oats
1 cup milk
1 egg, beaten
¼ cup canola oil
¾ cup brown sugar
½ teaspoon baking soda
½ teaspoon salt
1 teaspoon baking powder
½ cup gluten-free oat flour
½ cup gluten-free flour mix*
½ teaspoon xanthan gum
1 cup blueberries

Combine oats and milk. Add egg and oil. In separate bowl, combine brown sugar, baking soda, salt, baking powder, oat flour, flour mix, and xanthan gum. Add dry mix to wet mix. Stir to moisten well. Add blueberries. Fill lined muffin cups, adding more blueberries on top if desired. Bake at 400 degrees for 20 minutes or until muffins test done with toothpick.

*GLUTEN-FREE FLOUR MIX

Combine 2 parts brown rice flour and 1 part tapioca starch. Mix well. Store in airtight container.

JULIE TROYER, Fredericksburg, Ohio

Almond Flour Banana Muffins

GLUTEN-FREE   **NO ADDED SUGAR**

4 ripe bananas, mashed
2 eggs, beaten
½ cup stevia blend
⅓ cup milk
¼ cup ground flaxseed
⅓ cup canola oil
1 teaspoon vanilla

1 cup oatmeal
1 cup almond flour
1 tablespoon baking powder
½ teaspoon salt
½ cup mini dark chocolate chips
½ cup chopped walnuts

In large bowl, mix together bananas, eggs, stevia blend, milk, flaxseed, oil, and vanilla. In separate bowl, mix oatmeal, almond flour, baking powder, and salt. Mix with banana mixture until just combined. Stir in chocolate chips and nuts. Spoon into prepared muffin tins. Bake at 350 degrees for 25 minutes.

Emma Byler, New Wilmington, Pennsylvania

Oatmeal Cinnamon Rolls

EGG-FREE GLUTEN-FREE NUT-FREE

1 cup gluten-free quick oats
2 cups boiling water
3 tablespoons butter
1 tablespoon sugar
¾ cup brown sugar
1½ teaspoons salt

2 tablespoons yeast dissolved
in ⅓ cup warm water
2 tablespoons butter, melted
½ cup brown sugar
2 teaspoons cinnamon

Mix oatmeal with boiling water and let stand 20 minutes. Add butter, sugar, ¾ cup brown sugar, salt, and dissolved yeast. Let dough rise to double in size. Roll out into rectangle. Brush with melted butter. Combine ½ cup brown sugar with cinnamon. Sprinkle onto dough. Roll up dough from long side and slice. Let slices rise in baking pan. Bake at 350 degrees for 20 minutes.

JOANN MILLER, Fredericktown, Ohio

Chocolate Chip Pumpkin Muffins

 DAIRY-FREE GLUTEN-FREE  REFINED SUGAR–FREE

1¾ cups gluten-free oatmeal
1 cup pumpkin or sweet
    potato puree
½ cup maple syrup
    or molasses
2 eggs
1 teaspoon vanilla
4 tablespoons coconut oil

1 teaspoon baking powder
½ teaspoon baking soda
½ teaspoon salt
1 teaspoon cinnamon
1 cup chopped nuts
½ cup gluten-free oatmeal
Chocolate chips

Blend all ingredients except nuts, ½ cup oatmeal, and chocolate chips in blender. Stir in nuts and ½ cup oatmeal. Fill muffin cups ⅔ full. Sprinkle chocolate chips on top. Bake at 350 degrees for 20 to 25 minutes.

Lela Brenneman, Montezuma, Georgia

Spiced Autumn Pumpkin Muffins

 DAIRY-FREE  GLUTEN-FREE

2 cups blanched almond flour
3 tablespoons coconut flour
1 teaspoon baking soda
2 teaspoons cinnamon
¾ teaspoon nutmeg
¼ teaspoon ground ginger
¼ teaspoon cardamom
¼ teaspoon ground cloves

¼ teaspoon sea salt
¾ cup pumpkin puree
⅓ cup maple syrup or honey
2 large eggs at room
    temperature
2 tablespoons coconut oil,
    melted
1 teaspoon vanilla

In bowl, combine almond flour, coconut flour, baking soda, cinnamon, nutmeg, ginger, cardamom, cloves, and salt. In another bowl, mix pumpkin, maple syrup, eggs, oil, and vanilla. Slowly add dry mixture to wet mixture, stirring until smooth. Line muffin tin with baking cups and fill cups ⅔ full with batter. Bake at 350 degrees for 25 minutes or until muffins test done with toothpick.

Joann Miller, Fredericktown, Ohio

Cappuccino Muffins

⅔ cup milk
2 tablespoons instant
   coffee granules
½ cup butter, melted
2 eggs, beaten
¾ cup honey
1 teaspoon vanilla

¼ cup cocoa powder
2½ teaspoons baking powder
1 teaspoon cinnamon
1¼ cups almond flour
½ cup oat flour
¼ cup coconut flour

Combine milk and coffee granules, stirring until dissolved. Add butter, eggs, honey, and vanilla. In separate bowl, combine cocoa powder, baking powder, cinnamon, almond flour, oat flour, and coconut flour. Add to liquid mixture, stirring until well mixed. Fill greased muffin tins ⅔ full. Bake at 375 degrees for 17 to 20 minutes or until muffins test done with toothpick. Serve with cream cheese spread.

Cream Cheese Spread

4 ounces cream cheese,
   softened
1 tablespoon honey
½ teaspoon instant coffee

½ teaspoon vanilla
¼ cup mini semisweet
   chocolate chips

Beat cream cheese until smooth. Add honey, instant coffee, and vanilla. Beat well. Mix in chocolate chips.

JULIA TROYER, Fredericksburg, Ohio

BREAKFAST

Nehemiah said, "Go and enjoy choice food and sweet drinks, and send some to those who have nothing prepared. This day is holy to our Lord. Do not grieve, for the joy of the LORD is your strength."

NEHEMIAH 8:10

CRUNCHY CEREAL

 EGG-FREE

2½ cups old-fashioned
  oatmeal
½ cup coarsely chopped
  unsalted dry-roasted
  peanuts
½ cup sesame seeds
½ cup sunflower seeds
½ cup nonfat dry milk

½ cup wheat germ
¼ cup brown sugar, honey,
  maple syrup, or white
  grape juice concentrate
2 teaspoons cinnamon
¼ cup oil (canola, safflower,
  or olive)
2 teaspoons vanilla

In large bowl, mix oatmeal, peanuts, sesame seeds, sunflower seeds, dry milk, and wheat germ. In another bowl, combine sugar, cinnamon, and oil, stirring until smooth. Stir into dry mixture. Spread on pan and bake at 300 degrees for 1 hour, stirring every 10 minutes. Remove from oven and sprinkle with vanilla once it is cold. Store in airtight container.

KATIE YODER, Utica, Ohio

Granola Cereal

 EGG-FREE GLUTEN-FREE NUT-FREE  REFINED SUGAR–FREE

4 cups gluten-free quick oats
4 cups gluten-free old-fashioned oats
2 cups unsweetened coconut
2 pinches salt

½ cup coconut oil
1 cup butter
¾ to 1 cup real maple syrup
2 teaspoons maple flavoring (optional)

Combine quick oats, old-fashioned oats, coconut, and salt; set aside. In medium saucepan, melt coconut oil, butter, and maple syrup over medium heat. Boil 5 minutes or until syrupy. Remove from heat; add flavoring. Pour over dry mixture and mix gently but thoroughly. Lightly pat into 2 large (13x18-inch) cookie sheets. Bake without stirring at 300 degrees for 1 hour or until golden. Switch pans on racks halfway through baking. Cool cereal completely before storing in airtight containers. Chunky and crunchy goodness.

MARY ANN YUTZY, Bloomfield, Iowa

Granola

 DAIRY-FREE EGG-FREE  GLUTEN-FREE REFINED SUGAR–FREE

8 cups gluten-free quick oats
⅔ cup slivered almonds
⅔ cup pecans
1 cup unsweetened coconut
½ cup flaxseed meal

½ cup raisins
⅓ cup honey
⅓ cup maple syrup
1⅛ cups olive oil

In large bowl, mix oats, almonds, pecans, coconut, flaxseed meal, and raisins. In small bowl, combine honey, maple syrup, and olive oil. Pour over dry mixture and mix well. Spread on baking sheets. Bake at 250 degrees for 2 hours, stirring every 20 minutes until crisp.

RUBY MILLER, Auburn, Kentucky

Nutritious Baked Oatmeal

 GLUTEN-FREE · NUT-FREE · REFINED SUGAR–FREE

3 eggs
¾ cup maple syrup
¾ cup butter
3¾ cups gluten-free oats
½ cup finely shredded coconut
2 tablespoons ground flaxseed

3 teaspoons baking powder
1 teaspoon salt
½ teaspoon cinnamon
2 cups milk
1 cup raisins, chopped apples, blueberries, or other fruit

Combine all ingredients and bake in 9x13-inch pan at 350 degrees for 45 minutes. Serve warm with milk.

K. Hertzler, West Salisbury, Pennsylvania

Blueberry Breakfast Porridge

 DAIRY-FREE · EGG-FREE · GLUTEN-FREE · NUT-FREE

2 cups water
½ cup blueberries
½ teaspoon coconut oil or ghee
½ cup creamy brown rice cereal

½ cup milk of choice
1 tablespoon sweetener to taste
½ teaspoon salt
Flaxseed

In saucepan, bring water, blueberries, and oil to boil. Whisk in cereal. Boil well; reduce heat and simmer. Add milk, sweetener, and salt; simmer at least 15 minutes until cereal is soft. Stir occasionally. Top with flaxseed to serve.

Diana Miller, Fredericktown, Ohio

Breakfast Cups

6 slices deli ham	6 eggs
Cheese	Salt and pepper
Salsa	Bacon bits (optional)

Line 6 greased muffin cups with ham. Add layer of cheese and salsa to each cup. Break egg into each cup. Sprinkle with salt and pepper. Bake at 350 degrees for 20 to 25 minutes until whites are set and yolks are still soft. Sprinkle with bacon bits if desired.

BETHANY MARTIN, Homer City, Pennsylvania

Breakfast Eggs

1½ cups shredded cheese	Salt and pepper
12 eggs or enough to fit in pan	½ to 1 cup ham, bacon, or other cooked meat

In well-greased 9x13-inch pan, sprinkle 1 cup cheese. Make slight indentions in cheese for eggs. Break eggs into indentions. Poke yolks to break, but do not stir. Sprinkle with salt and pepper. Top with meat and remaining cheese. Bake at 350 degrees for 20 to 30 minutes. Can be prepared and put in refrigerator overnight for easy breakfast casserole.

MRS. RAY HERSHBERGER, Scottville, Michigan

JANETTE KUEPFER, Kincardine, Ontario

QUICHE (KÈSH)

 GLUTEN-FREE NUT-FREE

CRUST:

1¼ cups gluten-free flour
½ teaspoon salt
½ teaspoon sugar

½ cup cold butter
¼ cup cold water

Mix flour, salt, and sugar. Cut in butter until crumbly. Mix in water to form dough. Roll out and place in pie pan. Prick with fork. Cover with parchment paper and fill with pie weights or dried beans for blind baking. Par-bake at 350 degrees for 15 minutes.

FILLING:

6 eggs, beaten
½ cup milk
1¼ cups shredded cheese
1 cup or more diced chicken
1 cup or more chopped
    broccoli

1 tablespoon Mrs. Dash
    seasoning
Salt to taste

Blend eggs and milk. Add cheese, chicken, and broccoli. Season with Mrs. Dash and salt. Pour into crust. Bake at 350 degrees for 40 to 55 minutes until well set.

MRS. JOSEPH J. SCHWARTZ, Salem, Indiana

ZUCCHINI OMELET

 GLUTEN-FREE LOW-CARB NUT-FREE SUGAR-FREE

6 slices bacon, cut into small
    pieces
1 small onion, chopped
3 small zucchinis, shredded

1 teaspoon salt
½ teaspoon pepper
8 eggs, beaten
1 cup grated cheese

In medium skillet, fry bacon and onion until browned; pour off grease. Add zucchini, salt, and pepper. Cover and simmer until zucchini is tender. Add eggs and cheese. Turn to brown on both sides.

EMMA BYLER, New Wilmington, Pennsylvania

Veggie Omelet

GLUTEN-FREE · **LOW-CARB** · **NUT-FREE** · **SUGAR-FREE**

2 tablespoons butter	2 green onions, sliced
1 cup chopped asparagus	8 eggs, well beaten
¼ cup chopped broccoli	⅓ teaspoon salt
¼ cup chopped cauliflower	Shredded cheese (optional)
2 tablespoons grated carrots	

Melt butter in skillet and sauté asparagus, broccoli, cauliflower, carrots, and onions until tender. Mix eggs and salt and pour over vegetables. Cover and cook over low heat until egg is set well. Top with cheese if desired.

K. Hertzler, West Salisbury, Pennsylvania

Fried Corn Mush

EGG-FREE · GLUTEN-FREE · NUT-FREE · SUGAR-FREE

4 cups water
2 cups roasted cornmeal
½ cup white rice flour
2 teaspoons salt

2 cups cold water
4 tablespoons browned butter

Bring 4 cups water to boil. Mix together cornmeal, rice flour, salt, and 2 cups cold water. Stir into heated water. Bring to boil. Simmer on low for several hours. Remove from heat. Add browned butter. Pour into greased 8x8-inch pan. Cool. Slice, dip into coating mixture, and fry in oil.

Coating Mixture:

¼ cup rice flour
¼ cup cornstarch

¼ cup tapioca starch
1 tablespoon potato starch

Combine all ingredients.

Julia Troyer, Fredericksburg, Ohio

STRAWBERRY CREPES

CREPES:

¾ cup almond flour

3 tablespoons tapioca flour

3 tablespoons sweetener of choice

½ teaspoon xanthan gum

½ teaspoon salt

4 eggs

2 tablespoons butter or coconut oil, melted

1½ teaspoons vanilla

⅔ cup milk or almond milk

Mix almond flour, tapioca flour, sweetener, xanthan gum, and salt. In small bowl, beat eggs. Add to dry mixture. Add butter, vanilla, and milk. Let rest 5 minutes. Pour ⅓ cup batter into greased skillet. Shake pan to flatten out as thin as desired. Cook on low for 1 to 2 minutes on each side. Store crepes in refrigerator.

FILLING:

2½ tablespoons powdered sugar or powdered sweetener

3 ounces cream cheese

⅓ cup Greek yogurt

¾ cup heavy cream

Sliced strawberries

Beat cream cheese and powdered sugar in bowl until smooth. Add yogurt and beat. In another bowl, beat cream until stiff. Fold into creamed mixture. Spread crepes with filling and line with sliced strawberries. Roll or fold crepe around filling.

MARY ELLEN WENGERD, Campbellsville, Kentucky

ALMOND FLOUR PANCAKES

1 cup blanched almond flour

2 tablespoons tapioca flour

¼ teaspoon pink salt

1 teaspoon baking powder

2 eggs

¼ cup almond milk

½ teaspoon vanilla

2 tablespoons oil

Mix all ingredients and fry each side until golden.

MATTIE YODER, Millersburg, Ohio

GINGERBREAD WAFFLES

EGG-FREE GLUTEN-FREE NUT-FREE REFINED SUGAR-FREE

⅔ cup mild baking molasses
⅓ cup butter, melted
1½ cups milk or other milk substitute
2 tablespoons apple cider vinegar
2 cups brown rice flour
½ teaspoon xanthan gum

½ teaspoon baking soda
2 teaspoons baking powder
2 teaspoons cinnamon
½ teaspoon ground ginger
¼ teaspoon ground cloves
¾ teaspoon salt

Preheat waffle iron. In large bowl, stir molasses and butter. Add milk and vinegar. In separate bowl, whisk together brown rice flour, xanthan gum, baking soda, baking powder, cinnamon, ginger, cloves, and salt. Add to molasses mixture, stirring just until combined. Bake waffles on heated iron until golden brown. Remove to warm oven rack until ready to serve. Serve with butter and fresh fruit. Makes 3 large waffles.

CRYSTAL ROPP, Kalona, Iowa

Cottage Cheese Pancakes

1 cup gluten-free quick oats
1 cup eggs
1 cup cottage cheese

2 teaspoons baking powder
¼ teaspoon stevia
Splash of vanilla

In blender, pulse oats until fine. Add remaining ingredients. Blend until smooth. Fry in butter until browned on both sides.

Loretta Petersheim, Mifflin, Pennsylvania

Cornmeal Pancake

1 cup cornmeal
2 tablespoons honey
1 teaspoon Real Salt
1 cup boiling water
1 egg

½ cup milk
2 tablespoons butter
½ cup rice flour
2½ teaspoons baking powder

Combine cornmeal, honey, and salt. Slowly stir in boiling water and let set, covered, for 10 minutes. In separate bowl, beat egg, milk, and butter. Add to cornmeal mixture. Add flour and baking powder, and stir into batter, being careful not to overmix. Fry on hot, greased griddle. Yields 10 to 12 pancakes.

Mattie Hochstetler, Keytesville, Missouri

Pancake Mix

GLUTEN-FREE NUT-FREE

12 cups cassava flour
¾ cup baking powder
4 cups powdered milk

2 tablespoons salt
¼ cup sugar (optional)

Combine cassava flour, baking powder, powdered milk, salt, and sugar; mix well. Store in airtight container.

TO MAKE PANCAKES:
2 eggs
1 cup water

2 tablespoons butter, melted, or oil
1½ cups pancake mix

Mix all ingredients and fry pancakes in hot skillet.

Note: Most any gluten-free flour (buckwheat, oatmeal, oat bran, rye, or cornmeal) can be used instead of cassava flour.

MRS. WOLLIE (MARY) MILLER, Belize

Buckwheat Pancakes

DAIRY-FREE NUT-FREE SUGAR-FREE

1 cup buckwheat flour
½ teaspoon salt
1 cup apple juice

1 teaspoon baking powder
1 egg, beaten
2 tablespoons olive oil

Beat all ingredients well. Pour batter onto hot greased pan, turning each pancake once. Makes 8 to 10 pancakes.

MRS. TOBY (MERIAM) BYLER, Watsontown, Pennsylvania

French Toast

¼ cup rice flour
2 teaspoons sugar
⅛ teaspoon salt

1 cup milk
3 eggs
9 slices gluten-free bread

Beat together flour, sugar, salt, milk, and eggs. Soak bread in egg mixture until saturated. Cook on hot, greased griddle until golden brown on both sides.

LAURA MILLER, Fredericktown, Ohio

Blueberry Topping

3 tablespoons cornstarch
1 cup white grape juice
1 quart fresh or frozen
   blueberries

¼ cup water
Pinch salt
½ teaspoon lemon juice
¼ teaspoon cinnamon

Stir cornstarch into juice. Meanwhile, in 1.5-quart saucepan, bring blueberries and water to boil. Stir in cornstarch mixture. Boil for 2 minutes, stirring constantly. Add salt, lemon juice, and cinnamon. Serve hot over pancakes or waffles.

MRS. TOBY (MERIAM) BYLER, Watsontown, Pennsylvania

Salads and Side Dishes

Heal me, LORD, and I will be healed; save me and
I will be saved, for you are the one I praise.

JEREMIAH 17:14

> *"Eat food. Not too much. Mostly plants."*
>
> —MICHAEL POLLAN,
> *In Defense of Food: An Euter's Manifesto*

RANCH DIP

1 cup sour cream
¼ cup real buttermilk
2 tablespoons mayonnaise
1 teaspoon nutritional yeast
¼ teaspoon garlic powder

¼ teaspoon onion powder
½ teaspoon dill weed
¾ teaspoon real salt
¼ teaspoon black pepper
½ teaspoon Parmesan cheese

Combine all ingredients and serve with vegetables.

MRS. RAY HERSHBERGER, Scottsville, Michigan

HOT BUFFALO CHICKEN DIP

1 (8 ounce) package cream
  cheese
6 ounces hot sauce
3 chicken breasts boiled and
  shredded

1 cup cheddar cheese
½ cup ranch dressing

Combine all ingredients in saucepan. Heat until cheese is melted. Serve with tortilla chips.

DENA M. SCHWARTZ, Decatur, Indiana

COLORFUL VEGETABLE DIP

EGG-FREE · **GLUTEN-FREE** · **NUT-FREE** · **SUGAR-FREE**

1 cup sour cream
1 (8 ounce) package cream
   cheese, softened
2 teaspoons dry ranch
   dressing mix

1 medium carrot, finely
   grated
1 sweet red pepper, finely
   chopped
Shredded cheese

Stir sour cream, cream cheese, dressing mix, carrot, and red pepper together and chill. Cover with shredded cheese when ready to use. Serve with fresh veggies, crackers, or chips.

LISA SCHWARTZ, Geneva, Indiana

CORN AND BEAN DIP

DAIRY-FREE   EGG-FREE   GLUTEN-FREE
NUT-FREE   SUGAR-FREE   VEGAN

2 (15 ounce) cans black beans, drained and rinsed

3 (15 ounce) cans whole kernel corn, drained

2 small green peppers, chopped

¼ cup finely chopped onion

2 tablespoons lemon juice

1 teaspoon salt

½ teaspoon pepper

1 teaspoon chili powder

1 teaspoon hot sauce

3 tablespoons red wine vinegar

⅓ cup vegetable oil

Combine all ingredients. Refrigerate until serving. Serve with chips or Mexican meal.

JULIA TROYER, Fredericksburg, Ohio

Avocado Chip Dip

EGG-FREE GLUTEN-FREE NUT-FREE SUGAR-FREE

1 pint cherry tomatoes, halved
4 ounces feta cheese crumbles
1 tablespoon olive oil
1½ tablespoons red wine vinegar

½ teaspoon garlic powder
¼ cup chopped red onion
1 tablespoon parsley
Salt and pepper to taste
3 avocados, chopped
Blue corn chips

Mix all ingredients except avocados and corn chips. Let set a few hours or overnight. Just before serving, toss in avocado. Serve with blue corn chips.

EMMA MILLER, Baltic, Ohio

Salsa Deviled Eggs

DAIRY-FREE GLUTEN-FREE NUT-FREE SUGAR-FREE

6 large hard-boiled eggs
¼ cup salsa
2 tablespoons mayonnaise
1 green onion, finely chopped

Dash salt
Dash pepper
Tortilla chips

Cut eggs in half lengthwise. Remove yolks. Set whites aside. In small bowl, mash yolks. Add salsa, mayonnaise, onion, salt, and pepper. Mix well. Spoon into egg whites. Refrigerate. Just before serving, place tortilla chip on each egg half.

MRS. AMOS B. EICHER, Monroe, Indiana

Bacon-Chicken Salad

 GLUTEN-FREE NUT-FREE

Dressing:

½ cup mayonnaise
5 tablespoons barbecue
 sauce
3 tablespoons chopped onion
½ teaspoon salt

½ cup sugar (or equivalent
 amount of preferred
 sweetener)
¼ teaspoon pepper
¼ teaspoon liquid smoke

Mix all ingredients well and refrigerate until ready to serve.

Salad:

1½ pounds boneless, skinless
 chicken breast
4 cups chopped lettuce
4 cups chopped spinach

2 tomatoes, diced
Shredded cheese
10 strips bacon, cooked
 and crumbled

Grill chicken then cut into bite-sized pieces, or cut raw chicken in cubes and stir-fry until done. Cool. In large bowl, mix lettuce and spinach. Top with tomatoes, cheese, bacon, and chicken. Serve with dressing.

Katie Miller, Arthur, Illinois

Healthy Cabbage Salad

 DAIRY-FREE EGG-FREE GLUTEN-FREE LOW-CARB SUGAR-FREE VEGAN

1 quart thinly sliced cabbage
2 tablespoons olive oil
2 tablespoons vinegar
½ to 1 teaspoon garlic salt

1 tablespoon nutritional
 yeast
2 tablespoons slivered
 almonds or sunflower
 seeds

Place cabbage in bowl. In small bowl, mix olive oil, vinegar, and garlic salt. Pour over cabbage and toss to coat. Sprinkle with nutritional yeast and slivered almonds.

This salad is still good left over.

Katie Petersheim, Mifflin, Pennsylvania

Cauliflower "Potato" Salad

 DAIRY-FREE GLUTEN-FREE LOW-CARB NUT-FREE SUGAR-FREE

1 medium head cauliflower,
  broken into small florets
¼ cup mayonnaise
2 tablespoons lemon juice
2 packages sugar substitute
  like Splenda

½ teaspoon dried mustard
3 green onions, chopped
Salt and pepper to taste

Cook cauliflower in salted water until tender. Rinse in cold water, drain, and pat dry. In large bowl, mix mayonnaise, lemon juice, sugar substitute, and mustard. Gently stir in cauliflower and onions. Season to taste. Optional additions include hard-boiled eggs, crumbled bacon, and cheese.

Mrs. David Kurtz, Smicksburg, Pennsylvania

Layered Salad 4 Ways

GLUTEN-FREE LOW-CARB NUT-FREE

Dressing:

½ cup mayonnaise
1 tablespoon vinegar

½ teaspoon salt
1 tablespoon sugar

Mix all well. Pick salad option with which to serve dressing. Adjust amounts of salad ingredients to your needs.

Salad 1:

Cut up lettuce or cabbage and arrange on plate. Put finely grated carrots on top followed by grated pickles, dressing, and grated hard-boiled eggs.

Salad 2:

Cut up lettuce and arrange on plate. Spread with dressing. Top with crushed pineapple and shredded cheese. Garnish with chopped nuts. For a fancy touch, chop maraschino cherries into quarters and sprinkle on top.

Salad 3:

Cut up lettuce and arrange on plate. Spread with dressing. Top with grated hard-boiled eggs, shredded cheese, and bacon bits.

Salad 4:

Layer chopped vegetables on plate—lettuce, red cabbage, cauliflower, broccoli, and radishes. Spread with dressing. Top with shredded cheese and crumbled bacon.

Anna M. Byler, Commodore, Pennsylvania

Grape Salad

EGG-FREE GLUTEN-FREE NUT-FREE NO ADDED SUGAR

1 pound seedless grapes
1 (8 ounce) package
   cream cheese

1 (8 ounce) carton sour cream
1 teaspoon vanilla
¼ cup powdered stevia blend

Wash grapes and remove stems. Set aside. Mix cream cheese, sour cream, vanilla, and stevia. Add grapes and mix well.

Emma Byler, New Wilmington, Pennsylvania

Rhubarb Salad

2 cups chopped rhubarb
2 tablespoons raw cane sugar
2 tablespoons red wine
vinegar
1 tablespoon olive oil
1 onion, chopped

¼ teaspoon salt
¼ teaspoon pepper
8 cups mixed lettuce, torn
½ cup feta cheese
¼ cup chopped walnuts
¼ cup raisins

Toss rhubarb and sugar. Let set 10 minutes. Spread evenly in 9x13-inch pan. Roast at 450 degrees for 5 minutes. Let cool for 10 minutes. In bowl, mix vinegar, oil, onion, salt, and pepper until well blended. Place lettuce, cheese, walnuts, and raisins in large bowl. Pour dressing over greens and mix. Just before serving, toss in rhubarb.

EMMA MILLER, Baltic, Ohio

Tomato Supreme Salad

3 to 4 tomatoes
2 small cucumbers
1 bell pepper
1 onion
1½ cups cubed cheese
1 tablespoon grated
Parmesan

Chopped fresh herbs
(parsley, chives, basil)
2 tablespoons olive oil
½ tablespoon vinegar
Pinch stevia
Salt and pepper to taste

Cube tomatoes, cucumbers, pepper, and onion. Combine in bowl and add cheese and Parmesan cheese. In another bowl, mix herbs, olive oil, vinegar, stevia, and salt and pepper. Toss with vegetables. Refrigerate until serving.

MARY ELLEN WENGERD, Campbellsville, Kentucky

SAUERKRAUT SALAD

 DAIRY-FREE EGG-FREE  GLUTEN-FREE NUT-FREE VEGAN

½ cup olive oil
⅔ cup white vinegar
⅓ cup water
1 teaspoon dried dill
¾ cup raw cane sugar
1 bag SnowFloss sauerkraut, drained

1 cup finely chopped red pepper
1 cup finely chopped celery
1 cup finely chopped onion
1 cup shredded carrot

Mix oil, vinegar, water, dill, and sugar until sugar is dissolved. Combine with sauerkraut, red pepper, celery, onion, and carrot. Marinate overnight. Store in refrigerator up to a week.

EMMA MILLER, Baltic, Ohio

Vegetable Slaw

GLUTEN-FREE · LOW-CARB · NUT-FREE · SUGAR-FREE

3 cups shredded cabbage
5 plum tomatoes, chopped
1 cup fresh broccoli pieces
1 cup chopped cauliflower
½ cup chopped red onion
½ cup fat-free sour cream

¼ cup reduced-fat
  mayonnaise
1 tablespoon cider vinegar
¾ teaspoon salt
¼ teaspoon pepper

In bowl, combine cabbage, tomatoes, broccoli, cauliflower, and onion. In small bowl, combine sour cream, mayonnaise, vinegar, salt, and pepper. Pour over vegetables and toss to coat evenly. Cover and refrigerate until well chilled.

ANNA MARY LAPP, Paradise, Pennsylvania

Layered Fruit Salad

EGG-FREE · GLUTEN-FREE · NUT-FREE · REFINED SUGAR–FREE

8 ounces light cream cheese
1 (6 ounce) carton plain
  nonfat Greek yogurt
1 tablespoon honey
1 teaspoon finely shredded
  orange peel
1 medium orange, peeled
  and sectioned

3 medium kiwifruit, peeled
  and sliced
1 medium mango, peeled,
  seeded, and cubed
1 cup fresh blueberries

In mixing bowl, beat cream cheese until smooth. Add yogurt and honey and beat. Stir in orange peel. Divide fruit among 6 serving dishes. Top with cream cheese mixture. Serve immediately or cover loosely and chill for up to 4 hours.

ESTER PEACHEY, Flemingsburg, Kentucky

Cottage Cheese Salad

 EGG-FREE GLUTEN-FREE SUGAR-FREE

2 small packages sugar-free
orange gelatin
1 (20 ounce) can crushed
pineapple
3 packs sweetener of choice

12 ounces cottage cheese
¾ cup chopped pecans
1 cup mini marshmallows

Mix gelatin according to box directions, but do not chill. In saucepan, bring pineapple and sweetener to boil. Add to gelatin. Stir in cottage cheese, pecans, and marshmallows. Chill.

DAVID C. P. SCHWARTZ, Galesburg, Kansas

Fruit Salad

 DAIRY-FREE EGG-FREE GLUTEN-FREE NUT-FREE VEGAN

1 tablespoon unflavored
gelatin or agar-agar
2 cups warm water
2 tablespoons stevia
1 orange, peeled and
chopped

1 apple, peeled and chopped
1 cup blueberries
1 cup chopped strawberries
1 cup raspberries
2 kiwi, peeled and chopped
1 cup cherries, halved

Dissolve gelatin in warm water. Add stevia. Stir well and chill until starting to set. Once chilled, stir in fruits. Chill to set.

SUSANNA MAST, Kalona, Iowa

Italian Mixed Vegetables

🥛 DAIRY-FREE 🥚 EGG-FREE 🌾 GLUTEN-FREE
👁 LOW-CARB 🥜 NUT-FREE 🍬 SUGAR-FREE 🌱 VEGAN

1 (24 ounce) package frozen
   California blend vegetables
¼ cup water
¼ cup reduced-fat Italian
   salad dressing

¼ teaspoon salt
¼ teaspoon basil
⅛ teaspoon oregano
½ teaspoon onion powder

Bring vegetables to boil in water heated in large nonstick skillet. Cover and cook for 12 minutes. Uncover and cook, stirring, until liquid is reduced. Add salad dressing, salt, basil, oregano, and onion powder. Cook and stir until heated through. Yields 6 servings.

ANNA MARY LAPP, Paradise, Pennsylvania

Green Bean Specialty

EGG-FREE · **GLUTEN-FREE** · **LOW-CARB** · **NUT-FREE** · **SUGAR-FREE**

1 small onion, sliced	2 to 3 pounds green beans
1 clove garlic, minced	Salt and pepper to taste
2 carrots, sliced	Fresh chives, chopped
2 tablespoons butter	Fresh parsley, chopped
2 tablespoons olive oil	2 tablespoons sour cream

In skillet, sauté onion, garlic, and carrots in butter and oil. Add beans, stirring often until vegetables are almost soft. Add salt and pepper, chives, and parsley. Steam until ready to serve. Stir in sour cream.

MARY ELLEN WENGERD, Campbellsville, Kentucky

BEANS AND BROCCOLI

EGG-FREE GLUTEN-FREE LOW-CARB NUT-FREE SUGAR-FREE

½ cup chopped onions
1 cup chopped fresh
  mushrooms
Butter

1 quart canned or fresh
  green beans
3 cups broccoli florets
Salt to taste

Sauté onions and mushrooms in butter until slightly browned. Add to green beans in medium saucepan and heat. In steamer, cook broccoli to desired tenderness. Add broccoli to beans and stir to combine. Salt to taste. Vegetable amounts can be adjusted to suit taste.

EDNA IRENE MILLER, Arthur, Illinois

ROASTED CAULIFLOWER

EGG-FREE GLUTEN-FREE LOW-CARB NUT-FREE SUGAR-FREE

3 tablespoons olive oil
½ teaspoon paprika
1 teaspoon garlic powder
¼ teaspoon salt
½ teaspoon pepper

1 large head cauliflower
¼ cup grated Parmesan
  cheese
2 tablespoons fresh
  parsley flakes

Toss olive oil, paprika, garlic powder, salt, and pepper with cauliflower. Spread on baking sheet covered with silicone or parchment paper. Sprinkle with Parmesan cheese and parsley. Bake at 425 degrees for 15 minutes or until browned.

MRS. RAY HERSHBERGER, Scottville, Michigan

Noodles

DAIRY-FREE · **GLUTEN-FREE** · **NUT-FREE** · **SUGAR-FREE**

2¼ to 2½ cups (about 12)
  whole eggs
2 cups tapioca starch
1 cup millet flour

1 cup rice flour
2 cups potato flour
1 teaspoon xanthan gum

Beat eggs. (If you want, eggs can be separated and more yolks can be added compared to whites.) Add tapioca starch, mixing well. Stir in millet flour. Stir in rice flour. Add up to 2 cups potato flour until dough is stiff. Knead until flour is worked in. Cut dough into 1½-inch balls. Put dough through noodle maker on setting #2 several times until dough handles nicely. Put through again on setting #4 or #5. Dry by ironing them or in dehydrator until edges start to curl. Turn over and dry on other side. Stack on tea towel to steam before cutting.

REBECCA E. STUTZMAN, Gilman, Wisconsin

Mashed Potatoes

DAIRY-FREE · **EGG-FREE** · **GLUTEN-FREE** · **NUT-FREE** · **SUGAR-FREE** · **VEGAN**

Potatoes
Salt
Unflavored nondairy
  coffee creamer

Butter substitute like I Can't
  Believe It's Not Butter

Cook potatoes in salted water until tender. Strain and save cooking water. Mash potatoes. Add creamer and whip. Add some potato water and whip to preferred consistency. Add butter substitute to taste.

KATIE YODER, Goshen, Indiana

Stuffed Mushrooms

 EGG-FREE GLUTEN-FREE LOW-CARB NUT-FREE SUGAR-FREE

2 packs fresh brown or
  white mushrooms
8 ounces cream cheese
Garlic salt

Grated Parmesan cheese
Sliced bacon, cut in half
Toothpicks

Carefully break out mushroom stems. Soften cream cheese and season with garlic salt and Parmesan cheese to taste. Put cream cheese mixture in plastic bag. Cut off one corner and pipe cream cheese mixture into mushroom cavities. Wrap each half slice of bacon around mushroom and secure with toothpick. Grill over medium/hot heat until bacon is done. Serve warm.

DEBBI MILLER, Belle Center, Ohio

Roasted Sweet Potato Cubes

5 to 6 cups cubed sweet
potatoes
Cooking spray
Grated Parmesan cheese

Seasonings of choice (dill
weed, garlic salt, onion
powder, black pepper)

Place sweet potato cubes in 9x13-inch pan. Spray lightly with cooking spray. Toss with spatula and spray again. Sprinkle generously with Parmesan cheese and seasonings. Toss to coat. Cover with foil and bake at 400 degrees for 30 to 40 minutes or until fork tender. Uncover. Turn off oven. Leave sweet potatoes in oven for 10 minutes to dry out a bit.

Mary Ellen Wengerd, Campbellsville, Kentucky

Sweet Potato Fries

1 pound sweet potatoes,
cut in strips
2 tablespoons extra-virgin
olive oil

1 teaspoon sea salt

Toss sweet potatoes in bowl with oil and salt. Arrange on baking sheet in single layer. Bake at 475 degrees for 20 to 25 minutes or until browned and crisp. Serve immediately.

Edna Irene Miller, Arthur, Illinois

Main Dishes

Whether you eat or drink or whatever you do, do it all for the glory of God.

1 Corinthians 10:31

"This is the ancient secret. This is the cycle of life. Fasting follows feasting. Feasting follows fasting. Diets must be intermittent, not steady. Food is a celebration of life. Every single culture in the world celebrates with large feasts. That's normal, and it's good. However, religion has always reminded us that we must balance our feasting with periods of fasting—'atonement,' 'repentance,' or 'cleansing.'"

–Dr. Jason Fung,
The Obesity Code: Unlocking the Secrets of Weight Loss

SAUSAGE AND CHEESE BITES

EGG-FREE · GLUTEN-FREE · NUT-FREE · SUGAR-FREE

1 pound gluten-free sausage (mild or hot)
2 cups shredded cheese or cheese substitute
¼ cup butter, melted
1¼ cups brown rice flour
1 tablespoon plus ½ teaspoon baking powder
½ teaspoon salt
½ teaspoon xanthan gum
Water as needed
Dipping sauces: mustard, ketchup, barbecue sauce, etc.

In large bowl, stir together sausage, cheese, butter, rice flour, baking powder, salt, and xanthan gum. Mix well. Add water gradually until soft and cohesive dough forms. Roll into small balls and place on 10x15-inch baking sheet. Bake at 350 degrees for 15 to 20 minutes or until browned and crusty. Serve warm with dipping sauce.

CRYSTAL ROPP, Kalona, Iowa

Wanda's Favorite Veggie Sandwich

2 slices gluten-free bread, toasted

Enough all-natural mayonnaise to cover both slices of toasted bread

1 slice tomato

4 slices cucumber

2 strips red, green, or yellow bell pepper

¼ cup alfalfa sprouts

¼ cup shredded yellow or white cheddar cheese

On each slice of bread, spread mayonnaise. Top one slice with veggies, sprouts, and cheese. Cover with other slice and enjoy healthy veggie sandwich.

WANDA E. BRUNSTETTER

Meatless Loaf

2 cups cooked, mashed beans of any dry variety

1½ cups bread or cracker crumbs

2 eggs, beaten

¼ cup chopped onions

½ teaspoon salt

1 cup ketchup or barbecue sauce

1 teaspoon Worcestershire sauce

Combine all ingredients and shape into 2 small loaves. Place in shallow baking dish. Top with your favorite sauce. Bake at 350 degrees for 35 minutes or shape mixture into patties and fry in oil.

LENA TROYER, Redding, Iowa

Cabbage Rolls

1 pound lean ground beef
1 onion, finely chopped
1 teaspoon Worcestershire
  sauce
½ cup long-grain rice

1 egg
Salt and pepper
32 cabbage leaves
1 can (11.5 ounces) tomato
  juice

Combine beef, onion, Worcestershire sauce, rice, egg, salt, and pepper. To remove leaves from head of cabbage, you can freeze cabbage and thaw or put cabbage in boiling water for a few minutes then put in cold water and peel off 4 to 5 leaves. Repeat process to peel more leaves. If outer leaves are dark green, put cabbage in boiling water for a few minutes to soften. Place rounded tablespoon of mixture on each cabbage leaf and roll up. Place cabbage rolls in roaster. Cover with tomato juice and bake at 300 degrees for 2 hours. Chop remaining cabbage and put on top of rolls if desired, or top with sauerkraut. Recipe makes 32 rolls.

CATHY LYNN KUEPFER, Ontario, Canada

MEAT LOAF

EGG-FREE · **GLUTEN-FREE** · **LOW-CARB** · **NUT-FREE** · **SUGAR-FREE**

1 pound ground beef chuck
½ cup skim milk
1 tablespoon onion flakes
½ teaspoon salt
¼ teaspoon pepper
¼ teaspoon ground sage

¼ teaspoon dry mustard
1 tablespoon Worcestershire sauce
½ cup chopped green pepper
1 teaspoon parsley flakes

Combine all ingredients and bake in greased loaf pan at 350 degrees for 1 to 1½ hours.

ADEL SCHMIDT, Carlisle, Kentucky

BAKED FISH

DAIRY-FREE · **EGG-FREE** · **GLUTEN-FREE** · **LOW-CARB** · **NUT-FREE** · **SUGAR-FREE**

Coconut or olive oil
Raw, unbreaded fish fillets
Dill

Parsley
Onion powder
Garlic powder

Pour small amount of oil in glass baking dish. Arrange fish fillets in single layer in pan. Sprinkle with dill, parsley, onion powder, and garlic powder to your taste. Bake at 350 degrees for 20 to 30 minutes. Serve with tartar sauce if desired.

KATIE MILLER, Arthur, Illinois

Grilled Fish

EGG-FREE **GLUTEN-FREE** **LOW-CARB** **NUT-FREE** **SUGAR-FREE**

Place each piece of fish on foil square. Add pat of butter and onion slice. Sprinkle with lemon juice. Fold foil to tightly close. Place on grill over indirect heat. Cook 10 to 15 minutes or until fish is opaque and cooked through.

EMMA BEILER, Delta, Pennsylvania

Simple Baked Chicken

DAIRY-FREE **EGG-FREE** **GLUTEN-FREE** **LOW-CARB** **NUT-FREE** **SUGAR-FREE**

Chicken legs	Pepper
Salt	Ground sage

Prepare leg quarters, as many as meet your family's needs. Place in single layer in 9x13-inch pan. Sprinkle liberally with salt, pepper, and ground sage. Bake at 400 degrees about 30 minutes until skin is crispy and meat juice runs clear (chicken must reach internal temperatue of 165 degrees). Drain on paper towel before serving.

BETHANY MARTIN, Homer City, Pennsylvania

Delicious Chicken

EGG-FREE **GLUTEN-FREE** **LOW-CARB** **NUT-FREE** **SUGAR-FREE**

Use as many pieces of chicken as you need. Brush boneless, skinless chicken breast halves with oil. Roll in crushed Snyder's "Wholey Cheese" gluten-free crackers. Fry or bake until done (chicken must reach internal temperatue of 165 degrees).

MRS. IDA MAE STAUFFER, Homer City, Pennsylvania

Barbecued Chicken

 DAIRY-FREE EGG-FREE  GLUTEN-FREE NUT-FREE

Chicken, bone-in pieces
Salt or Tender Quick
    Meat Cure
4 tablespoons ketchup
4 tablespoons brown sugar

2 tablespoons Worcestershire
    sauce or coconut aminos
5 tablespoons water
1 tablespoon lemon juice
½ teaspoon mustard

Sprinkle chicken pieces with salt and place in container or bag. Refrigerate overnight. In saucepan, blend and heat ketchup, brown sugar, Worcestershire sauce, water, lemon juice, and mustard. Dip chicken in sauce and place in roasting pan. Pour remaining sauce over top. Cover pan with foil. Bake at 350 degrees for 1½ hours or until chicken tests done.

Mrs. Jonas Gingerich, Howard, Ohio

Herb Roasted Chicken

1 whole chicken (1½ to 1¾
    pounds)
4 tablespoons butter, melted
1 tablespoon lemon juice
½ teaspoon oregano

½ teaspoon rosemary
½ teaspoon sage
½ teaspoon sea salt
¼ teaspoon pepper

Cut chicken in half. Arrange chicken skin-side up in roasting pan. In small bowl, combine butter, lemon juice, oregano, rosemary, sage, salt, and pepper. Brush onto chicken. Roast at 450 degrees about 20 minutes until juices run clear (internal temperatue should reach 165 degrees). Broil 6 inches from heat for 3 minutes to crisp skin.

EDNA IRENE MILLER, Arthur, Illinois

Honey Mustard Chicken

2 pounds boneless, skinless
  chicken thighs
Salt
½ cup prepared mustard
¼ cup honey or maple syrup

2 tablespoons vinegar
½ teaspoon salt
¼ teaspoon pepper
1 tablespoon organic
  cornstarch

Sprinkle chicken with salt on all sides. Layer chicken in baking dish. Mix mustard, honey, vinegar, ½ teaspoon salt, pepper, and cornstarch. Pour over chicken. Bake covered at 450 degrees for 40 minutes or until done.

RACHEL D. MILLER, Millersburg, Ohio

Peanut Butter Chicken

1¼ pounds chicken breast
Oil
2 teaspoons cornstarch
1 cup chicken broth
¼ cup peanut butter

2 tablespoons soy sauce
  or coconut aminos
½ teaspoon salt
¼ teaspoon pepper
Cooked rice

Cut chicken into bite-size pieces and stir-fry in oil until done, about 10 to 15 minutes. Mix cornstarch, chicken broth, peanut butter, soy sauce, salt, and pepper. Pour over chicken. Cook until thick. Serve over rice.

MRS. RAY HERSHBERGER, Scottsville, Michigan

CURRY AND RICE

 DAIRY-FREE EGG-FREE GLUTEN-FREE NUT-FREE SUGAR-FREE

2 tablespoons olive oil
1 clove garlic, minced
1 teaspoon grated ginger
3 boneless, skinless chicken breasts, cut into bite-size pieces
1 (13.5 ounce) can of unsweetened coconut milk
2 to 4 tablespoons red curry paste

¾ cup chicken broth
5 ounces snow peas, chopped
2 lemon grass stalks, bruised
Salt and pepper to taste
1 tablespoon chopped cilantro
Cooked rice

In large skillet, heat olive oil and stir-fry garlic and ginger for 30 seconds. Turn down heat to medium-high and add chicken. Cook 5 minutes until chicken is no longer pink. Stir in coconut milk, curry paste, chicken broth, peas, and lemon grass. Bring to boil. Reduce heat and simmer for 10 minutes. Remove lemon grass. Season with salt and pepper. Garnish with cilantro. Serve over rice.

LORETTA PETERSHEIM, Mifflin, Pennsylvania

SLOW-COOKER CHICKEN STIR-FRY

 DAIRY-FREE EGG-FREE  GLUTEN-FREE
 LOW-CARB NUT-FREE  REFINED SUGAR–FREE

4 pounds chicken breasts, cubed
2 pounds stir-fry vegetables
½ cup water
½ cup low-sodium soy sauce or coconut aminos
4 tablespoons rice vinegar

2 teaspoons extra-virgin olive oil or sesame oil
4 garlic cloves, minced
2 tablespoons ginger
2 teaspoons honey or maple syrup

Add chicken and vegetables to slow cooker. In small bowl, mix water, soy sauce, vinegar, olive oil, garlic, ginger, and honey. Pour over chicken and vegetables. Cook on low for 3 to 5 hours or on high for 2 to 4 hours.

ROSANNA PETERSHEIM, Mifflin, Pennsylvania

Unique Chicken Stew

DAIRY-FREE · EGG-FREE · GLUTEN-FREE · LOW-CARB · NUT-FREE · SUGAR-FREE

4 medium skinless, boneless
  chicken pieces
6 cups cubed potatoes
1 cup sliced carrots
½ cup chopped celery
½ cup chopped onion

2 cups chopped cabbage
4 cups chopped broccoli
3 cups chopped cauliflower
Salt and pepper to taste
Lemon pepper to taste

Dice chicken into 1-inch squares. Place in 6-quart kettle with a little water and cook for 20 minutes. Add potatoes, carrots, celery, onion, cabbage, broccoli, and cauliflower. Add water to almost cover all ingredients. Cook until vegetables are tender. Add salt, pepper, and lemon pepper to taste.

KATIE SCHMIDT, Carlisle, Kentucky

Wild Rice Casserole

2 tablespoons cornstarch
1 cup water
¼ cup reduced-sodium
  soy sauce
1 teaspoon reduced-sodium
  chicken bouillon granules
2 cups sliced celery
1 medium onion, halved
  and sliced

1 cup sliced fresh
  mushrooms
2 tablespoons canola oil
2 cups shredded cabbage
1 (8 ounce) can sliced
  water chestnuts
2 cups cooked wild rice

Combine cornstarch, water, soy sauce, and bouillon until blended. Set aside. In nonstick skillet, sauté celery, onion, and mushrooms in oil for 8 minutes. Add cabbage and sauté 3 minutes more or until cabbage is tender. Stir in water chestnuts. Stir cornstarch mixture well and pour over vegetables. Bring to boil. Cook and stir over medium heat for 2 minutes or until thickened. Stir in rice. Pour into 8x11-inch baking dish coated with nonstick cooking spray. Cover and bake at 350 degrees for 30 minutes or until heated through. Yields 8 servings.

Anna Mary Lapp, Paradise, Pennsylvania

Quick Jambalaya

EGG-FREE　NUT-FREE　SUGAR-FREE

1 tablespoon oil
½ cup chopped onion
½ cup chopped green pepper
2 cups cooked, chopped
　chicken
2 cups cooked rice or
　macaroni

1 (15 ounce) can kidney
　beans, drained and rinsed
1 cup salsa
1 teaspoon thyme
1 teaspoon salt
½ teaspoon pepper
Shredded cheese

Heat oil in skillet. Fry onion and pepper until tender. Add chicken, rice, kidney beans, salsa, thyme, salt, and pepper. Simmer 15 minutes. Top with cheese and serve.

SALOMIE E. GLICK, Howard, Pennsylvania

Southwest Skillet Supreme

GLUTEN-FREE　NUT-FREE　SUGAR-FREE

2 pounds ground beef
1 teaspoon oregano
1 teaspoon salt
2 teaspoons chili powder
1 (16 ounce) can refried
　or pinto beans
3 (15 ounce) cans tomato
　sauce

1½ cups shredded
　cheddar cheese
Tortilla chips
2 cups shredded lettuce
2 tomatoes, diced
1 (4 ounce) can sliced black
　olives, drained
Sour cream

Brown meat. Add oregano, salt, chili powder, beans, and tomato sauce. Simmer 5 to 10 minutes. Pour onto large serving tray. Sprinkle on cheese. Arrange chips around edge of serving tray. Garnish with lettuce, tomatoes, olives, and small dollops of sour cream. Serves 8.

DIANA MILLER, Fredericktown, Ohio

Mexican Lasagna

1 bag gluten-free
   tortilla chips
2 cups cottage cheese
1 cup cheddar cheese
1 egg
1½ pounds ground beef
1 teaspoon salt
1 teaspoon pepper
1 package taco
   seasoning mix

1 quart tomato juice
Miracle Whip salad
   dressing (optional)
Lettuce
Onions
Tomatoes
Cheese

Cover bottom of 9x13-inch pan with layer of slightly crushed tortilla chips. Mix together cottage cheese, cheddar cheese, and egg, and put on top of chips. Put another layer of slightly crushed chips on top of cheese mixture. Brown ground beef and add salt, pepper, taco seasoning, and tomato juice. Spread on top of chips and bake at 300 degrees for 30 to 40 minutes. Top with Miracle Whip if desired. Sprinkle on lettuce, onion, tomatoes, and cheese. Yields 6 to 8 servings.

SARAH KUEPFER, Milverton, Ontario, Canada

Spaghetti Pie

6 ounces black bean
   spaghetti, cooked
⅓ cup grated Parmesan
   cheese
3 egg whites, well-beaten
1 pound ground beef
½ cup chopped onion
15 ounces tomato sauce

Pinch of stevia
1 teaspoon oregano
½ teaspoon garlic salt
1 cup 1 percent fat cottage
   cheese
½ cup mozzarella cheese
   (optional)

Drain cooked spaghetti. Stir in Parmesan cheese and egg whites. Press into lightly greased 10-inch pie pan to form crust. Brown ground beef. Drain. Rinse with hot water to remove grease. Drain. Add onion, tomato sauce, stevia, oregano, and garlic salt. Heat thoroughly. Spread cottage cheese into crust. Top with meat mixture. Sprinkle with mozzarella. Bake at 350 degrees for 20 minutes.

MRS. RAY HERSHBERGER, Scottville, Michigan

Zucchini Lasagna

1 pound ground beef or
   turkey
¼ cup chopped onion
1 (15 ounce) can tomato sauce
1 teaspoon sea salt
½ teaspoon oregano
½ teaspoon basil
¼ teaspoon pepper
4 medium zucchinis

1 cup regular or low-fat
   cottage cheese
1 egg, beaten
3 tablespoons gluten-free
   flour or thickener of choice
2 cups shredded part-skim
   mozzarella cheese, divided
Sea salt

Brown beef and onions. Add tomato sauce, salt, oregano, basil, and pepper. Bring to boil. Simmer 5 minutes. Slice zucchini lengthwise into ¼-inch slices. In small bowl, combine cottage cheese and egg. Place half zucchini slices in 9x13-inch pan. Sprinkle with half flour and additional salt. Top with cheese mixture and half of meat. Layer on remaining zucchini slices and flour, and sprinkle with salt. Spread with 1 cup cheese and top with remaining meat. Bake covered at 375 degrees for 1 hour until heated through and zucchini is tender. Remove cover and top with remaining 1 cup cheese. Return to oven until cheese is melted.

EDNA IRENE MILLER, Arthur, Illinois

Sweet Potato and Turkey Sausage Hash

DAIRY-FREE · EGG-FREE · GLUTEN-FREE · NUT-FREE

2 medium potatoes, diced
1 medium sweet potato, diced
7 ounces smoked turkey sausage, halved lengthwise and sliced ½-inch thick
1 small green pepper, chopped
1 medium onion
1 tablespoon parsley
⅓ teaspoon pepper

Lightly coat shallow baking pan with oil or cooking spray. Place potatoes and sweet potatoes in pan and toss to coat in oil. Bake at 400 degrees for 20 minutes until tender and lightly browned, turning once. Meanwhile, in large nonstick skillet, cook sausage, pepper, and onion for 8 to 10 minutes or until tender, stirring occasionally. Add in potatoes, parsley, and pepper.

ESTER PEACHEY, Flemingsburg, Kentucky

Sausage Zucchini Casserole

GLUTEN-FREE · LOW-CARB · NUT-FREE · SUGAR-FREE

6 cups finely shredded zucchini
1 teaspoon salt
4 eggs
½ cup Parmesan cheese
¼ cup coconut flour
1 garlic clove, minced
2 cups shredded cheddar cheese, divided
1 pound bulk Italian sausage, browned
2 (8 ounce) cans sliced mushrooms, drained

Place zucchini in colander lined with cheesecloth. Sprinkle with salt and drain for 30 minutes. Gather up sides of cloth and squeeze out as much liquid as possible. Combine zucchini, eggs, Parmesan cheese, coconut flour, garlic, and 1 cup shredded cheddar. Press on bottom of greased 9x13-inch pan. Bake at 350 degrees for 18 minutes. Remove from oven and layer on sausage, mushrooms, and remaining cheddar. Bake for 12 to 15 minutes more. Serves 8.

ROSANNA PETERSHEIM, Mifflin, Pennsylvania

Simple Pizza Rice Casserole

2 pounds ground beef
  or turkey
1 teaspoon Italian seasoning
¼ teaspoon garlic powder
1 teaspoon salt
1 pint tomato sauce
1½ cups uncooked brown rice

2 eggs
4 cups water
1 cup chopped onion
Desired toppings
  (mushrooms, olives,
  peppers, etc.)
Cheese (optional)

Brown ground beef. Add Italian seasoning, garlic powder, and salt. Stir in tomato sauce. In greased 9x13-inch pan, spread uncooked rice on bottom. In bowl, mix eggs with water and pour over rice. Distribute meat mixture over rice. Sprinkle onions and other desired toppings over meat. Top with cheese. Bake at 350 degrees for 1¼ hours.

Susanna Mast, Kalona, Iowa

Vera Mast, Kalona, Iowa

Rice Pizza

1½ pounds sausage
Onion, chopped
3 cups cooked rice
8 ounces cream cheese,
  softened

1 cup sour cream
1 quart pizza sauce
Sliced mushrooms
Pepperoni
Mozzarella cheese

Fry sausage with onion. In bowl, mix rice, cream cheese, and sour cream. Put rice mixture in greased 9x13-inch pan. Top with sausage and pizza sauce. Layer on mushrooms and pepperoni. Bake at 350 degrees for 30 minutes. Top with mozzarella and bake until cheese melts.

Josephine Schmidt, Carlisle, Kentucky

CAULIFLOWER PIZZA CRUST

GLUTEN-FREE · **LOW-CARB** · **NUT-FREE** · **SUGAR-FREE**

1 head cauliflower,
  cut in 1- to 2-inch pieces
¼ cup olive oil
2 eggs, beaten
½ teaspoon salt

1 teaspoon Italian seasoning
⅓ teaspoon garlic powder
4 cups grated mozzarella
  cheese

Steam cauliflower. Strain into cheesecloth and press out as much liquid as possible. Beat or mix until cauliflower is rice sized. Put in large frying pan over medium heat and stir often for about 10 minutes until dry. Spread on sheet pan to cool. Put in bowl and add olive oil, eggs, salt, Italian seasoning, and garlic power. Mix well. Add mozzarella and mix. May need to use hands to incorporate cheese. Spread evenly and thinly on greased sheet pan. Press together. Bake at 450 degrees for 20 minutes then broil until cheese looks slightly toasted. Add preferred pizza toppings (i.e., sauce, meats, and cheese). Return to oven until toppings heat and melt.

ESTHER L. MILLER, Fredericktown, Ohio

Zucchini Crust Pizza

GLUTEN-FREE · **LOW-CARB** · **NUT-FREE** · **SUGAR-FREE**

4 cups grated zucchini
1 teaspoon salt
1 cup shredded cheese
2 eggs
⅓ cup flour
½ teaspoon oregano
½ teaspoon basil
¼ teaspoon pepper

1 tablespoon olive oil
¾ cup shredded cheese
1 pound sausage, browned
8 thick slices Roma tomatoes
Other toppings of choice
   (mushrooms, onions,
   peppers)
¼ cup shredded cheese

Sprinkle zucchini with salt and let stand at least 10 minutes. Drain into cloth and squeeze out as much liquid as you can. In bowl, mix 1 cup shredded cheese, eggs, flour, oregano, basil, and pepper until moist dough forms. Gently blend in zucchini. Form into greased or parchment-lined 12-inch pizza pan, pressing to make rim around edges. Bake at 375 degrees for 20 minutes.

Brush crust with olive oil. Sprinkle with ¾ cup cheese and browned sausage. Arrange tomato slices and add other toppings of choice. Top with ¼ cup shredded cheese. Bake at 400 degrees for 10 to 15 minutes until cheese is melted and bubbly.

SHARON MILLER, Auburn, Kentucky

BEEF AND BARLEY SOUP

1¼ pounds steak, cut into
  bite-size pieces
1 tablespoon butter
1 pint beef broth
5 cups water

¾ cup barley
1 (10 ounce) package frozen
  mixed vegetables
Salt and pepper to taste

In large saucepan, sauté steak in butter until browned. Stir in beef broth, water, and barley. Simmer until barley is tender. Stir in mixed vegetables. Cook until just tender. Season with salt and pepper. Serve with crackers.

ANNA M. BYLER, Commodore, Pennsylvania

FAT-BURNING SOUP

1 large head cabbage,
  chopped
6 onions, chopped
2 (28 ounce) cans diced
  tomatoes in juice
5 carrots, sliced

1 bunch celery, diced
2 green peppers, chopped
1 package Lipton onion soup
  mix
Salt and pepper to taste
Beef bouillon if desired

Place cabbage, onions, tomatoes, carrots, celery, and peppers in pot. Cover with water. Boil for 10 minutes. Reduce heat and simmer until vegetables are tender. This soup can replace 1 meal per day for weight loss or maintenance. Can be frozen in meal-sized portions.

MRS. IDA MAE STAUFFER, Homer City, Pennsylvania

Leek Soup

8 large leeks
3 onions
3 to 4 tablespoons butter
2 quarts chicken broth

8 potatoes, sliced
Chicken seasoning to taste
Milk

Clean and slice leeks and onions. Sauté in butter. Add broth and potatoes. Flavor to taste with chicken seasoning. Cook 20 to 25 minutes until potatoes are soft. Cool then blend in blender. Add milk to thin to your liking. Blend. Serve hot or cold.

ANNA M. BYLER, Commodore, Pennsylvania

Cheddar Ham Chowder

2 cups water
2 cups cubed potatoes
½ cup sliced carrots
½ cup sliced celery
¼ cup chopped onion
1 teaspoon salt
¼ teaspoon pepper

¼ cup butter
¼ cup rice flour
2 cups milk
2 cups shredded cheddar
  cheese
2 cups frozen corn
1½ cups diced, cooked ham

In large saucepan, bring water, potatoes, carrots, celery, onion, salt, and pepper to boil. Reduce heat; cover and simmer 8 to 10 minutes or until vegetables are just tender. Remove from heat. Do not drain. Meanwhile, in another saucepan, melt butter and blend in rice flour. Add milk. Cook and stir until thickened. Add cheese and stir until melted. Stir into vegetables and return to heat. Add corn and ham. Heat thoroughly and serve.

LAURA MILLER, Fredericktown, Ohio

Wanda's Hearty Lentil Soup

 DAIRY-FREE EGG-FREE GLUTEN-FREE NUT-FREE  SUGAR-FREE

2 cups dried lentils,
  washed and drained
2 medium carrots, sliced
1 cup chopped cabbage
16 ounces stewed tomatoes
¼ cup chopped onion

1 teaspoon sea salt
½ teaspoon freshly
  ground pepper
8 to 10 cups all-natural
  beef broth

Combine all ingredients in large kettle and cook until vegetables and lentils are tender, about 45 minutes to an hour.

Wanda E. Brunstetter

Garlic Soup

 EGG-FREE GLUTEN-FREE LOW-CARB NUT-FREE SUGAR-FREE

26 cloves garlic (approx.
  2 heads), unpeeled
2 tablespoons olive oil
Sea salt
12 cloves garlic (approx.
  1 head), peeled
2 tablespoons butter
2¼ cups sliced onion
½ teaspoon cayenne pepper

1 heaping teaspoon turmeric
½ cup fresh diced ginger or
  1 tablespoon ginger powder
1½ teaspoons thyme
3½ cups vegetable broth
½ cup milk
Salt and pepper to taste
4 lemon wedges

Place unpeeled garlic cloves in small glass baking dish. Add olive oil. Sprinkle with salt and toss to coat. Cover baking dish tightly with foil and bake at 350 degrees for 45 minutes until garlic is golden brown and tender. Cool and squeeze garlic from peels into small bowl. In bowl, smash raw peeled garlic cloves; set aside.

In large saucepan, melt butter over medium heat. Add onion, cayenne, turmeric, ginger, and thyme. Cook until onions are translucent, about 6 minutes. Add roasted and raw garlic to onions and cook 3 minutes. Add broth and cover and simmer until garlic is tender, about 20 minutes. Working in batches, puree soup in blender until smooth. Return to saucepan, stir in milk, and season to taste with salt and pepper. Squeeze juice of 1 lemon wedge into each bowl when serving. Serves 4.

Mary Petersheim, Apple Creek, Ohio

DESSERTS

Eat honey, my son, for it is good; honey from the comb is sweet to your taste. Know also that wisdom is like honey for you: If you find it, there is a future hope for you, and your hope will not be cut off.

PROVERBS 24:13–14

"The doctor of the future will no longer treat the human frame with drugs, but rather will cure and prevent disease with nutrition."

—THOMAS EDISON

WANDA'S EASY APPLE CRISP

EGG-FREE **GLUTEN-FREE** **NUT-FREE** **REFINED SUGAR–FREE**

6 golden delicious apples, peeled and thinly sliced
1 cup coconut sugar
1 cup gluten-free flour

1 teaspoon cinnamon
1 cube salt-free butter, cut into chunks

Place apple slices in greased 8x8-inch baking dish. In bowl, crumble together coconut sugar, gluten-free flour, cinnamon, and butter. Pour crumbs over apple slices and bake at 350 degrees for 40 to 45 minutes. Note: If crumb mixture appears too dry, add small amount of water or lemon juice. Serve plain or with all-natural ice cream or whipped cream.

WANDA E. BRUNSTETTER

Wanda's Tasty Blueberry Crisp

EGG-FREE • GLUTEN-FREE • NUT-FREE • REFINED SUGAR-FREE

5 cups fresh or frozen
   blueberries
1¼ cups coconut sugar,
   divided
2 tablespoons instant tapioca
½ cup water

1 teaspoon lemon juice
½ cup butter, melted
1 cup gluten-free flour
1 cup gluten-free quick oats

Combine berries, ¾ cup coconut sugar, tapioca, water, and lemon juice. Pour into greased 9x13-inch baking dish. In bowl mix butter, ½ cup coconut sugar, flour, and oats. Sprinkle over blueberry mixture. Bake at 350 degrees for 40 minutes. Serve plain or with all-natural ice cream or whipped cream.

WANDA E. BRUNSTETTER

Baked Apples

DAIRY-FREE • EGG-FREE • GLUTEN-FREE
NUT-FREE • REFINED SUGAR-FREE • VEGAN

2 cups water
1 cup maple syrup
1 teaspoon cinnamon
3 slightly rounded
   tablespoons Clear Jel

⅓ cup water
Apples, peeled, halved,
   and cored

In saucepan, heat 2 cups water and maple syrup. In bowl, mix cinnamon, Clear Jel, and ⅓ cup water. Add to saucepan mixture. Bring to boil, stirring well. Fill greased 9x13-inch pan with peeled apple halves. Pour sauce over apples. Bake at 350 degrees for 30 to 40 minutes until apples are soft. Serve with whipped cream.

JULIA TROYER, Fredericksburg, Ohio

CLASSIC CHOCOLATE PUDDING

EGG-FREE **GLUTEN-FREE** **NUT-FREE**

1 cup soy or almond milk, divided

2 tablespoons cornstarch

1½ tablespoons cocoa powder

Pinch salt

¼ teaspoon liquid lecithin (optional)

3 tablespoons sweetener of choice

1 tablespoon cold butter (optional)

½ teaspoon vanilla

In small saucepan, heat ¾ cup milk over medium heat until milk just starts to simmer. Meanwhile, combine ¼ cup milk, cornstarch, cocoa, salt, and lecithin. Mix well until mixture is completely smooth. Stir into hot milk in thin stream, whisking constantly until pudding is thick and bubbly. Remove from heat and add sweetener, butter, and vanilla. Stir until butter is fully incorporated. Serve pudding hot, or cover and refrigerate. Makes 2 servings.

CRYSTAL ROPP, Kalona, Iowa

Chocolate Avocado Mousse

DAIRY-FREE EGG-FREE GLUTEN-FREE LOW-CARB
NUT-FREE SUGAR-FREE VEGAN

2 ripe avocados
½ cup or less cocoa powder
¼ to ½ cup unsweetened
  almond milk
⅛ teaspoon salt

Pinch stevia or 2 to 6
  tablespoons sugar
  equivalent
1 teaspoon vanilla

Puree all ingredients until smooth. Refrigerate to chill before serving.

Mrs. Ray Hershberger, Scottville, Michigan

Overnight Double Chocolate Chia Pudding

EGG-FREE GLUTEN-FREE NUT-FREE

1¼ cups organic chocolate
  milk
1 tablespoon agave syrup
1 teaspoon organic vanilla

1 tablespoon organic cocoa
  powder
¼ cup organic chia seeds

In mason jar, mix milk, agave, and vanilla with fork. Add cocoa and mix thoroughly.
Add chia seeds and mix. Refrigerate for 8 hours. Stir mixture and enjoy. For extra
delight, top with Greek yogurt and berries.

Vera Mast, Kalona, Iowa

Strawberry Chia Pudding

EGG-FREE GLUTEN-FREE LOW-CARB NUT-FREE

3 cups strawberry puree
½ cup chia seeds
1½ teaspoons vanilla
2 cups Greek yogurt

¼ cup Simple Sweet or
 sweetener of choice
⅔ cup cream

Stir together strawberry puree and chia seeds. Refrigerate overnight. Add vanilla, yogurt, sweetener, and cream. Serve.

MARY ELLEN WENGERD, Campbellsville, Kentucky

Pumpkin Pie Pudding

DAIRY-FREE EGG-FREE GLUTEN-FREE
LOW-CARB SUGAR-FREE VEGAN

1 cup raw cashews, soaked
 overnight and drained
1½ cups pumpkin puree
½ cup sweetener
2 teaspoons cinnamon
3 tablespoons organic
 lemon juice

½ teaspoon ginger
½ teaspoon nutmeg
½ teaspoon vanilla
½ teaspoon sea salt
½ teaspoon xanthan gum
6 tablespoons refined
 coconut oil

Blend all ingredients in blender until smooth. Refrigerate until cold and set.

ROSANNA PETERSHEIM, Junction City, Ohio

PUMPKIN GELATIN

3 cups water

2 tablespoons honey

1 cup bone broth

2 tablespoons unflavored
gelatin

1 cup cooked pumpkin puree

½ teaspoon cinnamon

Bring water to boil and cool slightly. Dissolve honey in water. At same time, bring broth to boil and cool slightly. Dissolve gelatin in broth. Let stand 10 minutes. Combine mixtures. Combine pumpkin and cinnamon. Stir into warm mixture. Chill fully before enjoying.

MOLLY KINSINGER, Meyersdale, Pennsylvania

FRUIT GELATIN

4 cups water

1 tablespoon honey

2 tablespoons unflavored
gelatin

½ to 1 cup fresh or frozen
berries or other fruit

Bring water to boil. Divide into 2 bowls and let cool slightly. Dissolve honey in one bowl and gelatin in the other. Stir gelatin and let set for 10 minutes. Combine contents of both bowls and stir. Add berries or fruit. Chill. Can serve with whipped cream.

MOLLY KINSINGER, Meyersdale, Pennsylvania

Raspberry Cheesecake Mousse

EGG-FREE · **GLUTEN-FREE** · **LOW-CARB** · **NUT-FREE** · **NO ADDED SUGAR**

1½ cups red raspberries, thawed if frozen
8 ounces cream cheese, softened
¼ teaspoon stevia
Dash vanilla
Pinch salt
¾ cup heavy whipping cream

Blend raspberries. Press through sieve to remove seeds. In separate bowl, beat cream cheese, stevia, vanilla, and salt until smooth. Gradually add raspberry puree and beat until smooth. Add cream and beat until thick and fluffy. Spoon into goblets and refrigerate until chilled. Garnish as desired.

MRS. RAY HERSHBERGER, Scottville, Michigan

Collagen Berry Whip

1 teaspoon unflavored
 gelatin
2 tablespoons cool water
2 tablespoons very hot water
½ teaspoon lecithin

2 pinches salt
1/16 teaspoon stevia
1½ tablespoons collagen
1 cup pureed berries or
 other fruit

In deep chilled bowl, soak gelatin in cool water. Stir in hot water. Add lecithin, salt, stevia, and collagen. Beat until whipped up. Chill. Stir in berries.

MOLLY KINSINGER, Meyersdale, Pennsylvania

Pineapple "Cheesecake"

1 (20 ounce) can crushed
 pineapple in its own juice
2 packages unflavored
 gelatin
½ cup hot water
1⅓ cups nonfat powdered
 milk

2 teaspoons vanilla
½ teaspoon butter flavoring
3 packages sugar substitute
½ teaspoon lemon juice

Drain pineapple. Place pineapple and half of drained juice in blender. Add gelatin and hot water. Add powdered milk, vanilla, butter flavoring, sugar substitute, and lemon juice. Blend 3 minutes. Pour into 10-inch round pan. Refrigerate at least 1 hour before serving.

ELIZABETH Y. MILLER, Middlefield, Ohio

CREAMY ESPRESSO CHEESECAKE

 GLUTEN-FREE

CRUST:

1½ cups almond flour
½ cup chopped pecans
¼ cup sugar

⅓ cup butter, melted
¼ teaspoon salt

Mix all ingredients. Press into 9-inch springform pan and bake at 350 degrees for 10 minutes. Cool.

FILLING:

3 (8 ounce) packages cream cheese
1½ cups sugar
1½ tablespoons ground espresso powder

1 teaspoon vanilla
½ teaspoon salt
3 eggs, lightly beaten
3 cups (24 ounce carton) sour cream

Beat cream cheese, sugar, espresso powder, vanilla, and salt. Add eggs and mix until just incorporated. Fold in sour cream. Pour over crust. Bake at 325 degrees for 1 hour and 15 minutes. Cool for an hour. Refrigerate several hours before serving.

KATIE YODER, Utica, Ohio

SUGAR-FREE ICE CREAM

 GLUTEN-FREE   NUT-FREE   SUGAR-FREE

3 eggs, beaten
6 cups milk
1 tablespoon unflavored gelatin

½ cup cold water
2 small packages sugar-free instant pudding
½ teaspoon salt

In saucepan, heat egg and milk to scalding, stirring constantly. In small bowl, dissolve gelatin in cold water. Add to milk; stir to dissolve. Remove from heat. Add pudding mix and salt. Chill. Freeze in ice cream maker.

MRS. JOHN H. MULLET, Cass City, Michigan

Fresh Fruit Dessert

EGG-FREE · **GLUTEN-FREE** · **NO ADDED SUGAR**

1 cup sour cream
1 (8 ounce) package cream
  cheese
1 (8 ounce) container whipped
  topping
2 cups plain yogurt

2 cups gluten-free pecan-
  raisin granola
Fresh fruit of choice (e.g.,
  sliced peaches, blueberries,
  strawberries)

Combine sour cream and cream cheese until smooth. Mix in whipped topping. Spread yogurt on bottom of large bowl or glass dish. Top with layer of granola, saving some for garnish. Spread on sour cream mixture. Top with fruit of choice. Garnish with granola.

CAROLINE SCHMIDT, Carlisle, Kentucky

STRAWBERRY "PRETZEL" DESSERT

 EGG-FREE · GLUTEN-FREE · LOW-CARB · NO ADDED SUGAR

CRUST:

1 cup almond flour
¾ cup chopped nuts
¼ teaspoon sea salt

2 tablespoons xylitol
2 drops liquid stevia
4 tablespoons butter, melted

Combine all ingredients and press into 8x8-inch pan. Bake at 350 degrees for 20 minutes until edges are golden brown. Cool completely before adding next layer.

PUDDING LAYER:

1 tablespoon unflavored
  gelatin
¼ cup cold water
¾ cup unsweetened almond
  milk

¾ cup half and half
1 teaspoon vanilla
½ cup pudding mix*
1 (8 ounce) package cream
  cheese

Dissolve gelatin in water. In saucepan, heat milk, half and half, vanilla, and pudding mix until very hot but not boiling. Remove from heat and immediately whisk in gelatin. Cool for 10 minutes. Pour into blender and add cream cheese. Blend well. Pour over cooled crust and chill for 1 to 2 hours or until completely set.

STRAWBERRY LAYER:

⅓ cup xylitol-sweetened
  strawberry gelatin
1 cup boiling water

1 cup cold water
1 pint sliced strawberries

Add gelatin to boiling water; stir until dissolved. Add cold water and strawberries. Cool until slightly thickened. Pour over already set pudding layer. Refrigerate until gelatin is completely set. Serves 9.

*PUDDING MIX

2 cups Sweet Mix sweetener
  (see page 157)
2 teaspoons Glucomannan or
  xanthan gum

4 scoops (or approximately
  1 cup) whey protein isolate
  powder
2 teaspoons sea salt

Combine all ingredients and store in airtight container.

ESTHER BORNTRAGER, Clark, Missouri

Peanut Butter Pie Dessert

Cashew Milk:

1½ cups raw cashews	⅛ teaspoon salt
3 cups water	¼ teaspoon xanthan gum

Combine cashews, water, and salt in heavy-duty blender. Blend for several minutes until mixture is very smooth. While blender is running, slowly sprinkle in xanthan gum and blend 1 more minute.

Pudding:

Cashew milk from above recipe, divided	1½ teaspoons vanilla
6 egg yolks	¼ teaspoon salt
½ cup sweetener (like erythritol)	

In shaker bottle, combine 1 cup cashew milk and egg yolks. Shake vigorously until smooth. In saucepan, place remaining cashew milk and sweetener and heat until partly warm. Whisk in egg mixture. Continue heating and whisking until thickened. Remove from heat. Add vanilla and salt. Whisk several times as pudding cools to prevent skin from forming on top. Pudding will thicken as it cools. Store in refrigerator until ready to use. Can adjust sweetener to taste.

Crust:

2 cups almond flour	¼ cup coconut sugar
½ cup coconut oil	¼ teaspoon salt
¾ cup finely chopped pecans	

Mix all ingredients until crumbly. Press ¾ of mixture or a bit more into bottom of 9x9-inch pan and partway up sides. Put remaining crumbs in pie pan. Bake at 350 degrees until starting to brown. Watch carefully. Cool.

Crumbs:

¾ cup peanut butter	1 teaspoon salt
1 cup almond flour	Reserved baked crumbs from above
¾ cup finely chopped pecans	
¾ cup coconut sugar	

Combine all ingredients with fork until crumbly. Refrigerate until ready to use.

To assemble: Spread ¾ of crumbs on top of cooled, baked crust in the 9x9-inch pan. Pour chilled pudding on top of crumbs. Sprinkle remaining crumbs on top. Chill until set.

Kathryn Troyer, Rutherford, Tennessee

PECAN PIE

REFINED SUGAR-FREE

3 eggs

1½ cups maple syrup

2 tablespoons butter, melted

2 tablespoons spelt flour

1 teaspoon vanilla

¼ teaspoon salt

1 cup pecans

1 (9 inch) unbaked pie shell

Beat eggs. Add maple syrup, butter, flour, vanilla, and salt. Stir in pecans. Pour into pie shell. Bake at 350 degrees for 30 minutes or until set and browned.

EDNA IRENE MILLER, Arthur, Illinois

STRAWBERRY PIE

EGG-FREE · **GLUTEN-FREE** · **REFINED SUGAR-FREE** · **NUT-FREE**

CRUST:

1½ cups gluten-free oat flour

⅓ cup coconut flour

½ cup butter or coconut oil, melted

Mix all ingredients, divide in half, and press into 2 pie plates. Bake at 350 degrees for 15 minutes or until golden. Cool.

FILLING:

1 (8 ounce) package cream cheese

8 ounces heavy cream, whipped

⅓ cup maple syrup or honey

Strawberries, sliced

Beat cream cheese, whipped cream, and maple syrup until smooth. Divide and spread over crusts. Top each pie generously with sliced strawberries.

Note: To make oat flour, blend quick oats until finely crushed. You can use all oat flour in the recipe, or you can replace coconut flour with almond flour.

LYDIANN GLICK, Howard, Pennsylvania

Almond Piecrust

EGG-FREE GLUTEN-FREE LOW-CARB SUGAR-FREE

1½ cups almond flour
3 tablespoons stevia

3 tablespoons butter, melted

Combine flour, stevia, and butter. Pat mixture into glass pie pan. Bake at 350 degrees for 8 minutes. Do not let crust brown. Cool.

Susanna Mast, Kalona, Iowa

Perfect Piecrust

EGG-FREE GLUTEN-FREE SUGAR-FREE

½ cup almond flour
½ cup coconut flour
½ cup arrowroot starch

¼ teaspoon salt
½ cup butter
¼ cup water

Combine almond flour, coconut flour, arrowroot starch, and salt in medium bowl. Cut in butter to form crumbly dough. Add water and mix until smooth dough is formed. If dough is still crumbly, add water 1 tablespoon at a time until dough becomes smooth. Shape into ball, wrap in plastic wrap, and refrigerate for ½ hour or overnight.

Remove dough from refrigerator and let sit for 10 to 15 minutes. This will make it easier to roll. Unwrap dough and place between 2 pieces of parchment paper. Press dough down slightly; then use rolling pin to roll dough into circle ¼ inch thick. Remove top sheet of parchment paper and smooth edges of dough to even out. Place 9-inch pan upside down on top of dough. Carefully turn dough and pie pan right-side up so dough is resting in pie pan and parchment is on top. Carefully press dough into pie pan and gently remove parchment paper. Use fingers to even out edges and smooth cracks until piecrust is formed in pan. Use fork to poke holes in bottom crust for even baking. Bake at 350 degrees for 20 minutes until firm to the touch and very lightly golden on edges. Allow crust to cool completely before filling.

Susie E. Kinsinger, Fredericktown, Ohio

CHOCOLATE COOKIE CRUST

DAIRY-FREE · **EGG-FREE** · **GLUTEN-FREE** · **LOW-CARB**
REFINED SUGAR–FREE · **NUT-FREE** · **VEGAN**

¼ cup refined coconut oil or butter
½ teaspoon molasses
1 cup blanched almond flour

⅔ cup sweetener of choice
⅛ teaspoon sea salt
¼ cup unsweetened cocoa powder

Melt butter in saucepan then remove from heat. Add molasses and stir until smooth. Add almond flour, sweetener, salt, and cocoa. Mix crumbs with fork. Use for pie or cheesecake crust by pressing mixture into bottom of greased pan.

Option: Sprinkle crumbly mixture on ice cream, pudding, mousse, etc.

CRYSTAL ROPP, Kalona, Iowa

GRAHAM CRACKER CRUST

DAIRY-FREE · **EGG-FREE** · **GLUTEN-FREE** · **LOW-CARB**
REFINED SUGAR–FREE · **VEGAN**

2 cups blanched almond flour
⅓ cup sweetener of choice
1 teaspoon cinnamon
¼ teaspoon sea salt

6 tablespoons refined liquid coconut oil
1 teaspoon molasses

Combine almond flour, sweetener, cinnamon, and salt. Stir in oil and molasses until well combined. Press mixture into greased pie plate and bake at 350 degrees for 12 to 15 minutes until slightly brown. Cool. Use for your favorite no-bake cheesecake or pie.

CRYSTAL ROPP, Kalona, Iowa

Cappuccino Frosting

4 ounces cream cheese, softened
1 tablespoon cocoa powder
1 teaspoon instant coffee

½ teaspoon vanilla
3 drops liquid stevia or a little honey

Mix all ingredients until smooth. Store in refrigerator.

JUDITH MILLER, Fredericktown, Ohio

Healthy Chocolate Frosting

1 cup olive oil
2 tablespoons arrowroot powder
½ cup carob powder

1 teaspoon vanilla
1 teaspoon salt
Sweetener of choice to taste, optional

Mix all ingredients until smooth, adding more or less carob for proper spreading consistency.

MARY PETERSHEIM, Apple Creek, Ohio

Cool Mint Frosting

½ cup whipped cream
1 drop peppermint oil
1 drop green food coloring (optional)

1 ounce cream cheese, softened

Beat all ingredients on low until well combined. Chill.

JUDITH MILLER, Fredericktown, Ohio

CHOCOLATE DATE CAKE

7.5 ounces unsweetened chocolate, finely chopped
½ teaspoon baking soda
1 tablespoon cocoa powder
1 teaspoon vanilla

1¼ cups pitted dates, finely chopped
¼ cup coconut oil
3 eggs
Chocolate chips (optional)

Put all ingredients in blender and mix well. Make sure dates and chocolate are chopped fine. There will be some small pieces. Pour into greased or parchment-lined 8x8-inch pan. Bake at 350 degrees for 25 to 30 minutes. Sprinkle chocolate chips on top before baking if desired.

LORETTA PETERSHEIM, Mifflin, Pennsylvania

SIMPLE CHOCOLATE CAKE

5 eggs, separated
½ cup cocoa powder
2 tablespoons tapioca flour or 4 tablespoons arrowroot powder

¼ cup oil
3 tablespoons very warm water
⅓ cup raw sugar

Separate eggs. In glass bowl, beat egg whites until stiff. In large bowl, mix yolks, cocoa, tapioca flour, oil, water, and sugar. Fold in egg whites. Pour into greased round cake pans. Bake at 300 degrees for 25 minutes. Serve with or without frosting.

SHARON MILLER, Auburn, Kentucky

Applesauce Cake

2 cups unsweetened
  applesauce
2 eggs
1 teaspoon baking soda
½ teaspoon salt
1 teaspoon baking powder
1 teaspoon cinnamon

½ teaspoon ground cloves
½ teaspoon nutmeg
1 teaspoon ginger
1 cup whole wheat flour
1 cup raisins
¼ cup chopped nuts

Combine applesauce and eggs. Add remaining ingredients. Mix well and spread in 8x8-inch pan. Bake at 350 degrees for 40 to 45 minutes.

JUDY ZIMMERMAN, East Earl, Pennsylvania

Bean Cake

2½ cups cooked black beans
6 eggs
¼ cup honey or ¼ teaspoon stevia
1 teaspoon vanilla
1½ teaspoons baking powder
1 teaspoon baking soda
1 teaspoon salt
¼ cup butter or other fat
½ cup shredded coconut
½ cup chopped nuts
¾ cup grated zucchini, carrot, or apple

Mash beans. Add remaining ingredients. Mix well. Pour into greased 9x9-inch pan. Bake at 350 degrees for 30 to 40 minutes until cake tests done.

LENA TROYER, Redding, Iowa

Black Bean Cake

1⅔ cups cooked black beans
5 eggs
½ teaspoon salt
½ cup honey
½ cup raw sugar
¾ teaspoon baking soda
1 tablespoon vanilla
6 tablespoons butter, melted
6 tablespoons carob powder (or 3 tablespoons cocoa powder plus 3 tablespoons brown rice flour)
1 tablespoon water

Put all ingredients in blender and blend until smooth. Bake in greased 9x9-inch or 8x11-inch pan at 350 degrees for 30 minutes or until cake tests done. Cool. Spread with icing.

ICING:

¾ cup peanut butter
½ cup coconut oil
3 tablespoons cocoa or carob powder
2 tablespoons honey
½ teaspoon stevia
1 teaspoon vanilla
Sprinkle of salt

In saucepan, combine all ingredients and melt over medium heat. Add more stevia if needed.

IDA MAST, Kalona, Iowa

Old-Fashioned Oatmeal Cake

1 cup gluten-free quick oatmeal

5 tablespoons butter

1½ cups boiling water

1 cup Sweet Mix (see page 157)

1¾ cups gluten-free baking blend

1 teaspoon blackstrap molasses

2 eggs

¼ teaspoon salt

2 teaspoons baking soda

2 teaspoons baking powder

1 teaspoon cinnamon

1 teaspoon vanilla

Mix oatmeal, butter, and boiling water. Let set to soften 5 minutes. Stir in remaining ingredients. Bake in greased 9x13-inch pan at 350 degrees for 30 to 35 minutes or until toothpick comes out clean.

Frosting:

½ cup butter

Pinch salt

⅔ cup Sweet Mix

1 teaspoon blackstrap molasses

½ cup unsweetened coconut

½ cup chopped nuts

In saucepan, bring butter, salt, Sweet Mix, and molasses to boil. Boil 3 minutes. Stir in coconut and nuts. Pour on top of hot cake. Broil until golden brown.

Mrs. Miriam Raber, Flat Rock, Illinois

SUNSHINE CAKE

 DAIRY-FREE LOW-CARB NUT-FREE SUGAR-FREE

This is as close to chiffon cake as low-carb can get. For maximum volume, make sure egg whites are at room temperature before whipping them.

1¾ cups Atkins baking mix
1 cup granular sugar
   substitute
¼ teaspoon salt
1 tablespoon grated
   orange rind
9 egg yolks

¾ cup cold water
½ cup vegetable oil
2 teaspoons vanilla
12 egg whites, room
   temperature
½ teaspoon cream of tartar

In large bowl, whisk baking mix, sugar substitute, salt, and orange rind. In separate bowl, combine yolks, water, oil, and vanilla. Slowly fold liquid mixture into dry mixture using rubber spatula. Mix well. In glass bowl, beat egg whites with cream of tartar until stiff. In 3 additions, fold egg whites into batter. Pour batter into ungreased tube pan. Bake at 350 degrees for 55 minutes until toothpick comes out clean. Cool upside down. To remove cake from pan, run knife around inside edge of pan.

MRS. DAVID KURTZ, Smicksburg, Pennsylvania

Turtle Cake

GLUTEN-FREE NUT-FREE

3 cups caramel bits
1 (14 ounce) can sweetened
  condensed milk
¼ cup butter
2 cups brown sugar
½ cup cocoa powder
1¼ cups brown rice flour
½ cup oil

1 teaspoon vanilla
3 eggs, beaten
½ cup sour cream or milk
2 teaspoon baking soda
¾ teaspoon xanthan gum
¾ cup tapioca starch
1 cup hot water
Chocolate chips

In saucepan, melt caramel bits in milk and butter over low heat. Set aside to cool. In mixing bowl, combine brown sugar, cocoa, and flour. Add oil, vanilla, eggs, sour cream, baking soda, xanthan gum, and tapioca starch. Beat well. Add hot water. Pour half of batter into greased baker's half-sheet pan. Bake at 350 degrees for 15 minutes. Cool 15 minutes. Pour caramel mixture over baked cake. Top with remaining cake batter. Sprinkle with chocolate chips. Bake another 25 minutes or until done.

JULIA TROYER, Fredericksburg, Ohio

Zucchini-Carrot Cake

DAIRY-FREE EGG-FREE GLUTEN-FREE SUGAR-FREE VEGAN

2½ cups gluten-free oat flour
1 tablespoon baking powder
1 teaspoon baking soda
2 teaspoons stevia
2 teaspoons cinnamon
½ teaspoon ginger
½ teaspoon allspice

½ teaspoon nutmeg
1 teaspoon salt
½ cup water
1 cup oil
2 cups grated zucchini
2 cups grated carrots
1 cup chopped nuts

Mix oat flour, baking powder, baking soda, stevia, cinnamon, ginger, allspice, nutmeg, and salt. Add water and oil. Mix well. Stir in zucchini and carrots. Add nuts. Pour into greased 8x12-inch pan. Bake at 350 degrees for 1 hour.

ESTHER L. MILLER, Fredericktown, Ohio

BLUEBERRY COFFEE CAKE

REFINED SUGAR-FREE

2 eggs
⅔ cup butter
1 teaspoon vanilla
1 tablespoon honey
2 cups oatmeal
1 cup whole grain flour
1 teaspoon salt
2 teaspoons baking soda
½ teaspoon cream of tartar
¾ teaspoon stevia
2 teaspoons baking powder
1 cup buttermilk
3 tablespoons applesauce
1 cup blueberries
1 cup chopped nuts

Cream eggs, butter, vanilla, and honey until fluffy. In separate bowl, mix oatmeal, flour, salt, baking soda, cream of tartar, stevia, and baking powder. Stir in buttermilk and applesauce. Mix in egg mixture. Fold in blueberries and nuts. Pour into greased cake pan.

TOPPING:

⅓ cup chopped nuts
¾ teaspoon cinnamon
⅓ cup whole grain flour
3 tablespoons butter
1 teaspoon honey

Mix nuts, cinnamon, and flour. Stir in butter and honey. Sprinkle over top of cake batter. Bake at 350 degrees for 40 to 45 minutes.

ESTHER MILLER, Keytesville, Missouri

Pink Cupcakes

1 (15 ounce) can white navy beans, drained and rinsed
5 large eggs
1 egg yolk
6 tablespoons coconut oil, softened
⅛ teaspoon stevia
1 tablespoon vanilla
6 tablespoons almond meal
½ teaspoon sea salt
½ teaspoon baking soda
1 teaspoon baking powder
8 drops red food coloring (optional)
½ cup coarsely chopped strawberries

Place beans in blender with eggs and egg yolk. Pulse on high until beans are smooth. In bowl, cream coconut oil and stevia. Add to bean mixture. Mix on medium speed. Add vanilla, almond meal, salt, baking soda, baking powder, and food coloring. Mix on medium speed. In bowl, fold mixture into strawberries. Spoon into lined cupcake pan. Bake at 350 degrees for 15 to 20 minutes. Allow cupcakes to rest 24 hours to allow the "bean" flavor to disappear.

Ruby Miller, Auburn, Kentucky

Avocado Brownies

1 ripe avocado
½ cup cocoa powder
2 eggs
1 cup coconut sugar or cane
    sugar, or ½ cup honey
¼ cup almond butter or
    peanut butter

1 teaspoon baking powder
1 teaspoon vanilla
¼ teaspoon sea salt
½ cup dark chocolate chips

In mixing bowl, mash avocado with fork until relatively smooth. Add cocoa, eggs, sugar, almond butter, baking powder, vanilla, and salt. Mix until smooth (can be done in food processor). Fold in chocolate chips. Grease 9x9-inch pan and line with parchment paper. Pour batter into prepared pan. Sprinkle additional chocolate chips on top if desired. Bake at 325 degrees for 45 minutes or until set. Cool brownies completely before cutting and serving.

ROSANNA PETERSHEIM, Mifflin, Pennsylvania

Black Bean Brownies

1½ cups black beans,
    rinsed and drained
4 eggs
¼ teaspoon baking soda
½ teaspoon baking powder
3 tablespoons coconut oil

⅓ cup cocoa powder
¼ teaspoon salt
2 teaspoons vanilla
Dash cayenne pepper
¼ cup honey

Place beans and eggs in blender and pulse until beans are smooth. Pour into mixing bowl and add remaining ingredients. Mix well. Pour into greased 9x9-inch baking pan. Bake at 350 degrees for 20 to 25 minutes or until toothpick comes out clean.

SHARON MILLER, Auburn, Kentucky

Chocolate Chip Cookie Bars

½ cup cold salted butter
1 cup almond flour
⅓ cup coconut flour
⅓ cup Gentle Sweet or Pyure
    sweetener or 1 cup sugar

½ cup collagen powder
½ teaspoon salt
1 teaspoon vanilla
⅔ cup sugar-free
    chocolate chips

In food processor combine all ingredients except for chocolate chips until mixture forms ball. Stir in chips. Press into 8x10-inch rectangle on top of parchment-covered baking sheet. Bake at 350 degrees for 18 to 20 minutes.

Mrs. Ray Hershberger, Scottville, Michigan

No-Bake Chewy Chocolate Bars

1 cup peanut butter or
    almond butter
⅔ cup honey
1 teaspoon vanilla
⅔ cup cocoa powder

2 cups shredded coconut
1 cup gluten-free oatmeal
½ to 1 cup mini chocolate
    chips
½ cup chopped pecans

Mix peanut butter, honey, vanilla, and cocoa. Add coconut and oatmeal. Taste for sweetness and add more honey if desired. Stir in chocolate chips and pecans. Spread mixture in buttered 9x9-inch pan. Refrigerate.

Diana Miller, Fredericktown, Ohio

BUTTERSCOTCH BROWNIES

GLUTEN-FREE

½ cup butter
2 cups brown sugar
1 teaspoon vanilla
3 eggs
1 cup rice flour

½ cup soy flour
2 teaspoons baking powder
½ teaspoon salt
1 cup finely chopped nuts

Cream butter and brown sugar. Add vanilla and eggs; beat lightly. In separate bowl, combine rice flour, soy flour, baking powder, and salt. Add to first mixture and blend well. Stir in nuts. Spread evenly in greased 9x13-inch pan. Bake at 350 degrees for 25 to 30 minutes or until top is light brown. Cool 10 to 15 minutes before cutting into bars. Yields 2 dozen.

EMMA A. HERSHBERGER, Apple Creek, Ohio

LEMON BARS

CRUST:

¾ cup coconut flour

3 tablespoons cane sugar

⅛ teaspoon salt

½ cup cold butter, cubed

1 large egg white

In bowl, combine coconut flour, sugar, and salt. Cut in butter until mixture becomes grainy. Add egg white and combine until dough is fully hydrated and forms pea-sized pieces. Press firmly into greased 8x8-inch pan. Bake at 325 degrees for 10 to 12 minutes until outer edges just begin to brown.

FILLING:

¾ cup lemon juice from 4 to 5 lemons

1 tablespoon lemon zest

1 teaspoon vanilla

4 large eggs

2 large egg yolks

¾ cup cane sugar

1 tablespoon coconut flour

3 tablespoons heavy cream powder or regular heavy cream

In medium bowl, whisk lemon juice, lemon zest, vanilla, whole eggs, and yolks. Add sugar, flour, and heavy cream powder. Whisk to combine. Pour filling over crust. Return to oven and bake at 325 degrees for 30 minutes or until filling has set. Chill bars at least 2 hours or overnight before serving.

ROSANNA PETERSHEIM, Mifflin, Pennsylvania

Susie-Q Bars

1½ cups cooked beans
2 cups gluten-free oatmeal
¾ cup unsweetened shredded
  coconut
2 teaspoons baking powder
¾ teaspoon baking soda
1½ cups chopped apples
1 cup blueberries

½ teaspoon cinnamon
1 teaspoon vanilla
2 eggs
1 cup coconut oil, melted
¼ cup agave or maple syrup
1 teaspoon salt
½ teaspoon stevia
½ cup nuts

Blend beans in blender until smooth. Mix in remaining ingredients. Pour into greased 10x15-inch pan. Bake at 350 degrees for 25 minutes until bars tests done.

Lena Troyer, Redding, Iowa

Peanut Butter Swirl Bars

1 cup peanut butter
⅔ cup butter
1½ cups brown sugar
1¼ cups cane sugar
5 eggs
4 teaspoons vanilla

2 cups brown rice flour
3 teaspoons baking powder
½ teaspoon salt
1 teaspoon xanthan gum
1 (12 ounce) bag semisweet
  chocolate chips

Cream peanut butter, butter, brown sugar, sugar, eggs, and vanilla. Stir in flour, baking powder, salt, and xanthan gum. Spread in jelly roll pan. Sprinkle chocolate chips on top. Bake at 350 degrees for 5 minutes. Use knife to swirl chocolate through dough. Bake for 30 minutes or until done.

Crystal Ropp, Kalona, Iowa

Pumpkin Bars

5 eggs
2 cups cane sugar
1 cup salad oil
1 cup pumpkin puree
2 cups brown rice flour

2 teaspoons baking powder
½ teaspoon salt
1 teaspoon baking soda
2 teaspoons cinnamon

Beat eggs thoroughly. Add sugar, oil, and pumpkin. Add flour, baking powder, salt, baking soda, and cinnamon. Spread in greased jelly roll pan. Bake at 350 degrees for 20 minutes. Frost when cooled if desired.

CRYSTAL ROPP, Kalona, Iowa

Chocolate Chip Cookies

1 cup plus 2 tablespoons
  butter, softened
3 cups, scant, brown sugar
⅓ cup oil
3 eggs
2 teaspoons vanilla
3 tablespoons hot water

¾ cup instant vanilla
  pudding mix
2¼ teaspoons baking soda
½ teaspoon sea salt
2 teaspoons xanthan gum
4¾ cups cookie flour mix*
3 cups chocolate chips

In mixing bowl, cream butter, brown sugar, and oil. Add eggs, vanilla, hot water, and pudding mix. Beat well. Add remaining ingredients, mixing well. Drop by spoonfuls onto cookie sheets and bake at 350 degrees for 10 to 11 minutes or until golden. Let set before removing from pans.

*COOKIE FLOUR MIX

2 cups white rice flour
1 cup tapioca starch
1½ cups oat flour

¼ cup potato starch or potato
  flour
¼ cup coconut flour

Combine all ingredients. Store in airtight container.

JULIA TROYER, Fredericksburg, Ohio

Chocolate Peanut Butter Oatmeal Cookies

2 cups peanut butter
2 cups butter, softened
1 cup Gentle Sweet
½ cup glycerin
1 teaspoon salt
2 teaspoons vanilla

4 eggs
3 cups twice-flaked oatmeal
3½ teaspoons baking soda
¾ cup chopped nuts
1 (12 ounce) package sugar-
free chocolate chips

Cream peanut butter and butter. Add sweetener, glycerin, salt, vanilla, and eggs. Beat. Stir in oatmeal, baking soda, nuts, and chocolate chips. Bake at 350 degrees for 10 to 12 minutes.

Rosanna Petersheim, Mifflin, Pennsylvania

Dark Chocolate Peanut Butter Cookies

 GLUTEN-FREE

20 ounces bittersweet chocolate chips, divided (at least 60 percent cocoa)
3 tablespoons butter
2 tablespoons creamy peanut butter
3 large eggs
1 cup sugar
1 teaspoon vanilla
½ cup sorghum flour
¼ teaspoon baking soda
¼ teaspoon xanthan gum
¼ teaspoon salt
1 cup finely chopped walnuts or peanuts

In medium bowl, microwave 8 ounces (heaping cup) chocolate chips, butter, and peanut butter on low power for 1 to 2 minutes or until melted (can also be melted in oven). Stir, set aside to cool. In large bowl, beat eggs, sugar, vanilla, flour, baking soda, xanthan gum, and salt with electric mixer on low speed until well blended. Beat in melted chocolate mixture until no flour streaks remain. Stir in walnuts and remaining chocolate chips. Dough will be soft. Cover and refrigerate 2 hours. Line 10x15-inch cookie sheet with parchment paper. Shape dough into 48 walnut-size balls. Place 12 balls 1½ inches apart on sheet. Bake at 375 degrees for 10 to 12 minutes, just until cookies are shiny and crust starts to crack. Cool cookies at least 2 minutes on baking sheet then transfer to cooling rack. Repeat with remaining dough or freeze balls up to one month and bake later. Yields 48 cookies.

They melt in your mouth!

Susie E. Kinsinger, Fredericktown, Ohio

Best-Ever Chocolate Chip Cookies

 DAIRY-FREE GLUTEN-FREE  REFINED SUGAR-FREE

1 egg
½ cup honey
1 cup peanut butter
1 teaspoon baking soda
1 cup chocolate chips

Combine all ingredients. Drop on cookie sheet with cookie scoop. Flatten slightly. Bake at 350 degrees for approximately 13 minutes. Let cool on pan for 2 minutes before removing.

Martha Troyer, Millersburg, Ohio

Gluten-Free Buttermilk Cookies

GLUTEN-FREE NUT-FREE

1 cup buttermilk
1 cup sugar
1 cup brown sugar
3 eggs, beaten
1 cup butter or lard
1 teaspoon baking soda

3 teaspoons baking powder
3¾ cups brown rice flour
½ teaspoon salt
⅓ cup cornstarch
1 teaspoon xanthan gum

Beat buttermilk, sugar, and brown sugar. Mix in beaten eggs and butter. Add baking soda, baking powder, rice flour, salt, cornstarch, and xanthan gum. Chill in refrigerator until cold. Roll dough into balls. Bake at 350 degrees for 10 minutes. Yields: 35 cookies.

CRYSTAL ROPP, Kalona, Iowa

Golden Diabetic Cookies

REFINED SUGAR-FREE

1 cup mashed pumpkin
⅓ cup oil
2 eggs
½ cup molasses
1 cup whole wheat flour
½ cup wheat germ
1 teaspoon baking soda

½ teaspoon salt
½ teaspoon cinnamon
½ teaspoon nutmeg
1 cup milk
1 cup raisins
½ cup walnuts or
   sunflower seeds

In large bowl, mix pumpkin, oil, eggs, and molasses. In small bowl, mix flour, wheat germ, baking soda, salt, cinnamon, and nutmeg. And to pumpkin mixture alternately with milk. Stir in raisins and walnuts. Drop by teaspoonfuls onto baking sheet. Bake at 350 degrees for 10 minutes. If batter is too thin, add oatmeal to thicken.

EMMA A. HERSHBERGER, Apple Creek, Ohio
MRS. IDA MAE STAUFFER, Homer City, Pennsylvania

Healthy Cookies

DAIRY-FREE · **EGG-FREE** · **GLUTEN-FREE** · **REFINED SUGAR–FREE** · **VEGAN**

2¾ cups almond flour
½ teaspoon baking soda
½ teaspoon salt
½ cup maple syrup

½ cup olive or coconut oil
1 tablespoon vanilla
¾ cup chocolate chips

Mix almond flour, baking soda, and salt. Add maple syrup, oil, and vanilla. Stir in chocolate chips. Drop by teaspoonfuls onto baking sheet, and bake at 350 degrees for 15 to 20 minutes. You can also bake bars in 9x13-inch pan, but they will need longer to bake.

KATIE SUE FISHER, New Holland, Pennsylvania

Fruit Cookies

DAIRY-FREE · **NO ADDED SUGAR**

½ cup chopped apple
½ cup chopped dates
1 cup raisins
1 cup water
⅓ cup oil
3 eggs
½ teaspoon salt

1⅓ cups whole wheat flour
  or 1½ cups white flour
1 teaspoon vanilla
1 teaspoon baking soda
1 teaspoon cinnamon
½ cup chopped walnuts

In saucepan, cook apple, dates, and raisins in water for 3 minutes. Cool. Add oil, eggs, salt, flour, vanilla, baking soda, and cinnamon. Mix well. Add walnuts. Mix well. Dough can be chilled before baking. Drop by tablespoonful on greased cookie sheet. Bake at 350 degrees for 15 minutes. Do not overbake. Store in cool place.

MRS. TOBY (MERIAM) BYLER, Watsontown, Pennsylvania

MARY STUTZMAN, West Salem, Ohio

Oatmeal Raisin Cookies

 GLUTEN-FREE

1 cup raisins
1 cup boiling water
1 cup butter
2 cups sugar or Sucanat*
2 eggs
1 teaspoon baking soda
1 teaspoon cinnamon
(optional)

3 cups gluten-free oatmeal
2 cups chopped nuts
2¼ cups gluten-free flour or
2 cups rice flour with
tapioca starch or
cornstarch
¾ teaspoon xanthan gum

Soak raisins in boiling water. Set aside. In bowl, mix butter, sugar, and eggs. Mix until creamy. Stir in baking soda and cinnamon. Add raisins with the water. (I like to blend raisins and water by chopping them up before adding.) Mix in oatmeal and nuts. Combine flour and xanthan gum and add to main mixture. Allow dough to set 30 minutes. Drop by teaspoonfuls onto baking sheet. Bake at 400 degrees for 8 to 10 minutes.

*Note: You can reduce sugar to 1¼ cups by adding ¼ teaspoon cream of tartar. Add cream of tartar with baking soda and cinnamon.

ESTHER L. MILLER, Fredericktown, Ohio

Peanut Butter Cookies

 DAIRY-FREE GLUTEN-FREE

1½ cups creamy
peanut butter
2 eggs

1 teaspoon vanilla
1 cup brown sugar

Combine all ingredients. Roll into balls and flatten on cookie sheet. Bake at 325 degrees for 8 to 12 minutes. Let set 2 minutes before removing from pan.

LYDIA MILLER, Loudonville, Ohio

Nut Cookies

GLUTEN-FREE

⅓ cup butter
1 cup sugar
1 egg
1 tablespoon safflower oil
1 scant cup white or
 brown rice flour

Pinch salt
1 teaspoon baking powder
½ to ¾ cup chopped nuts
 of choice

Cream butter, sugar, egg, and oil. Add flour, salt, and baking powder. Mix in nuts. Form into 1-inch balls and place on greased baking sheet. Bake at 350 degrees for 15 to 20 minutes. Remove from oven and immediately dust with sugar (optional). This makes a crisp cookie.

EMMA A. HERSHBERGER, Apple Creek, Ohio

Oat Sandwich Cookies

DAIRY-FREE   GLUTEN-FREE   REFINED SUGAR–FREE   NUT-FREE

½ cup coconut oil
¼ cup honey
⅓ cup brown sugar
1 egg
1 teaspoon vanilla
1 teaspoon cinnamon
¼ teaspoon nutmeg

½ teaspoon salt
¾ teaspoon baking soda
¼ cup tapioca starch
1 cup brown rice or oat flour
2 cups gluten-free quick oats
Frosting of choice

Cream coconut oil, honey, and brown sugar. Add egg and vanilla. In separate bowl, combine cinnamon, nutmeg, salt, baking soda, tapioca starch, and flour. Combine with creamed mixture. Add oats. Mix well. Drop by teaspoonfuls onto baking sheet. Bake at 375 degrees for 8 to 10 minutes. Cool. Sandwich 2 cookies with frosting in between.

RUBY MILLER, Auburn, Kentucky

TRIPLE CHOCOLATE BISCOTTI

DAIRY-FREE   **GLUTEN-FREE**   **LOW-CARB**   **SUGAR-FREE**

1¾ cups almond flour
¼ cup cocoa powder
⅓ cup erythritol
½ teaspoon baking powder
½ teaspoon xanthan gum
⅛ teaspoon salt
¼ cup coconut oil, melted

1 large egg
1 teaspoon vanilla (or instant
   coffee dissolved in
   1 teaspoon water)
Stevia sweetened chocolate,
   melted

Whisk together almond flour, cocoa, sweetener, baking powder, xanthan gum, and salt. Stir in melted coconut oil, egg, and vanilla until dough forms. Turn dough onto greased baking sheet. Form into long, low log about 4x10 inches. Bake at 325 degrees for 25 minutes. Remove from oven and cool a little before cutting into 16 even slices. Reduce oven temperature to 250 degrees. Place slices cut-sides down on baking sheet and bake 15 minutes. Turn slices over and bake an additional 15 minutes. Let cool completely. Dip part of each slice in melted chocolate. Cool to harden.

KATHRYN TROYER, Rutherford, Tennessee

Maple Walnut Biscotti

DAIRY-FREE GLUTEN-FREE LOW-CARB SUGAR-FREE

2 cups almond flour	½ teaspoon xanthan gum
¼ cup erythritol	¼ cup coconut oil
¼ cup Stevia in the Raw (equivalent to ¼ cup sugar)	1 large egg, lightly beaten
1 teaspoon baking powder	¾ teaspoon maple flavoring
	½ cup walnut pieces, toasted

Whisk together almond flour, erythritol, stevia, baking powder, and xanthan gum. Stir in oil, egg, and flavoring. Mix until dough comes together. Stir in walnuts. Turn dough onto greased baking sheet. Form into long, low log about 4x10 inches. Bake at 325 degrees for 25 minutes or until lightly browned. Remove from oven and cool a little before cutting into 15 even slices. Reduce oven heat to 250 degrees. Place slices cut-sides down on baking sheet and bake 15 minutes. Turn slices over and bake additional 15 minutes. Let cool completely. Glaze.

GLAZE:

¼ cup powdered erythritol	½ teaspoon maple flavoring
1½ tablespoons almond milk	

Combine all ingredients until smooth.

KATHRYN TROYER, Rutherford, Tennessee

SNACKS and CANDY

*Have mercy on me, LORD, for I am faint;
heal me, LORD, for my bones are in agony.*

PSALM 6:2

> *"Don't eat anything incapable of rotting."*
>
> **–MICHAEL POLLAN,**
> *In Defense of Food: An Eater's Manifesto*

NO-BAKE ENERGY BITES

DAIRY-FREE · **EGG-FREE** · **GLUTEN-FREE** · **REFINED SUGAR-FREE**

1 cup gluten-free oats
⅔ cup toasted coconut flakes
½ cup natural peanut butter
½ cup ground flaxseed or
   wheat germ
⅓ cup honey or
   ¼ teaspoon stevia

1 teaspoon vanilla
½ cup chocolate chips
   (optional)
3 tablespoons chia seeds
   (optional)

In medium bowl, thoroughly combine all ingredients. Let chill in refrigerator for 30 minutes. Roll into balls. Store in airtight container in refrigerator for up to 1 week.

DENA M. SCHWARTZ, Decatur, Indiana

VERA MAST, Kalona, Iowa

Famous Fiber Balls

 DAIRY-FREE EGG-FREE GLUTEN-FREE REFINED SUGAR-FREE

2 cups shredded coconut
3 cups gluten-free oats
1 cup flaxseed meal
1⅛ to 1½ cups peanut butter
1 to 1¼ cups honey

1 to 2 tablespoons vanilla
1½ cups chocolate chips
2 tablespoons chia seeds (optional)
¾ cup raisins (optional)

Toast coconut in oven until lightly browned. Combine coconut with remaining ingredients and shape into balls. Store in airtight container in refrigerator for up to 1 week.

Ada J. Mast, Kalona, Iowa
This is our family's favorite healthy energy snack.

Mrs. Eli (Mary) Miller, Andover, Ohio

Protein Snack Balls

 DAIRY-FREE EGG-FREE GLUTEN-FREE REFINED SUGAR-FREE

⅔ cup raw honey
½ cup coconut oil or butter, melted
¼ cup cocoa powder
½ cup raw sunflower or pumpkin seeds
½ cup nuts (slivered almonds, chopped walnuts, etc.)

Handful of chocolate chips and/or raisins
1 cup natural peanut butter
3½ cups organic rolled oats
½ cup chia seeds

Mix all ingredients well and use cookie scoop to shape into balls. Put on wax paper–covered cookie sheet. Refrigerate until firm. Store in container in refrigerator.

Katie Miller, Arthur, Illinois

Simple No-Bake Energy Bars

 DAIRY-FREE EGG-FREE  GLUTEN-FREE  NO ADDED SUGAR

2¼ cups chocolate chips

1½ cups unsweetened peanut butter

¾ cup coconut oil or butter

Pinch salt

2 cups sunflower seeds

2 cups unsweetened coconut flakes

2 cups finely chopped walnuts

½ cup raisins

Combine all ingredients and press into 9x13-inch pan. Refrigerate. Cut into bars. Individually wrap or bag each bar. Can be frozen.

RACHEL D. MILLER, Millersburg, Ohio

Oatmeal Energy Bars

DAIRY-FREE | **GLUTEN-FREE** | **NO ADDED SUGAR**

3 cups gluten-free oats
½ cup shredded coconut
½ cup chocolate chips
½ cup dried cranberries
¼ cup flaxseed
¼ cup chopped nuts

1 cup unsweetened
  applesauce
½ cup peanut butter
2 eggs
¼ teaspoon salt

Mix oatmeal, coconut, chocolate chips, cranberries, flaxseed, and nuts. Stir in applesauce, peanut butter, eggs, and salt. Pour into greased 8x8-inch pan. Bake at 325 degrees for 15 to 17 minutes until golden.

JUDY ZIMMERMAN, East Earl, Pennsylvania

Peanut Butter–Chocolate Granola Bars

DAIRY-FREE | **EGG-FREE** | **GLUTEN-FREE** | **REFINED SUGAR-FREE**

⅔ cup chopped almonds
¾ cup chopped cashews
1½ cups gluten-free oats
⅓ cup ground flaxseed
½ cup mini chocolate chips

½ cup dried cranberries
⅓ cup raisins
1 cup peanut butter
½ cup honey
½ teaspoon sea salt

Place almonds and cashews in large bowl. Add oats, flaxseed, chocolate chips, cranberries, and raisins. Mix together. In microwave-safe bowl, melt peanut butter. Stir in honey and salt. Allow mixture to cool slightly so it won't melt chocolate. Pour peanut butter mixture over dry mixture. Fold mixtures together with spatula until dry ingredients are coated. Press into parchment-lined 8x8-inch pan. Cut into at least 12 bars. Store in airtight container in refrigerator up to 2 weeks or at room temperature up to 10 days.

LORETTA BRUBAKER, Farmington, Missouri

Spiced Granola Bars

1 cup gluten-free oats
¼ cup dried cranberries
¼ cup sunflower seeds
¼ cup shredded coconut
¼ cup chopped nuts
2 tablespoons cocoa powder
1 teaspoon cinnamon
1 teaspoon ginger
½ teaspoon salt
¾ cup applesauce
1 tablespoon blackstrap molasses
1½ teaspoons vanilla

Combine all ingredients and pour into greased 8x8-inch pan. Bake at 325 degrees for 15 to 17 minutes.

JUDY ZIMMERMAN, East Earl, Pennsylvania

Arrowroot Crackers

3 cups arrowroot starch
2 cups cassava flour
2½ teaspoons salt
2 teaspoons baking powder
Heavy cream

Mix arrowroot starch, cassava flour, salt, and baking powder. Add just enough cream until dough is soft. Press into cookie sheet and cut into pieces. Bake at 400 degrees for 20 minutes until golden.

MRS. WOLLIE (MARY) MILLER, Belize

Homemade Cheese Wafers

EGG-FREE · **NUT-FREE** · **SUGAR-FREE**

4-ounce block sharp cheese
1½ cups spelt flour
¾ teaspoon salt

Dash red pepper
½ cup butter, softened

Grate cheese into bowl. Sift flour over cheese. Mix in salt and red pepper. In separate bowl, cream butter until fluffy. Add to cheese mixture. Knead until smooth ball forms. Refrigerate 1 hour. Shape into 1-inch rolls, slice ¼-inch thick, and place on baking sheet. Bake at 400 degrees for 8 to 10 minutes. Yields 6 dozen wafers.

MATTIE PETERSHEIM, Junction City, Ohio

Roasted Chickpeas

2 cups cooked chickpeas
2 tablespoons olive oil
1 tablespoon lemon juice
2 teaspoons onion powder

1 teaspoon ground rosemary
½ teaspoon salt
¼ teaspoon pepper

Toss all ingredients together. Roast on sheet pan at 350 degrees for 25 to 35 minutes, stirring often.

Mrs. Landis, Broolhead, Wisconsin

Microwaved Potato Chips

DAIRY-FREE **EGG-FREE** **GLUTEN-FREE** **NUT-FREE** **SUGAR-FREE** **VEGAN**

3 medium potatoes
¼ cup olive oil

1 teaspoon salt

Layer 3 paper towels on microwave-safe plate. Set aside. Scrub potatoes and cut into 1/16-inch-thick slices. Brush slices on both sides with olive oil and lightly sprinkle with salt. Arrange on plate in single layer. Microwave on high 3 minutes. Flip chips over and microwave 2 to 3 minutes until chips are dry. Cool.

ESTHER MARTIN, Fleetwood, Pennsylvania

Sweet Potato Chips

DAIRY-FREE **EGG-FREE** **GLUTEN-FREE** **NUT-FREE** **VEGAN**

Sweet potatoes
Coconut oil

Salt

Slice sweet potatoes very thin. In fryer, heat coconut oil to 400 degrees. Deep fry potatoes until no longer soft, but do not let them get dark. Drain on paper towel. Sprinkle with salt and/or other seasonings of choice.

IVAN YODER, Junction City, Ohio

Simple Healthy Chocolate

DAIRY-FREE **EGG-FREE** **GLUTEN-FREE** **REFINED SUGAR–FREE** **NUT-FREE**

½ cup coconut oil or butter
½ cup cocoa powder

¼ cup honey

In saucepan, heat oil, cocoa, and honey to melt. Pour into molds or pan.

For variation, add peanut butter, nuts, crispy rice cereal, or coconut. *Note:* Coconut oil gets sticky at room temperature.

JOSEPHINE SCHMIDT, Carlisle, Kentucky

Chocolate Almond Cups

1 cup coconut oil
1 cup cocoa powder
1½ cups almond butter
½ cup maple syrup

2 droppers liquid stevia
½ teaspoon salt
2 teaspoons vanilla

In saucepan over low heat, blend coconut oil with cocoa powder. Stir in almond butter and mix well. Add maple syrup, stevia, salt, and vanilla. Mix well. Put paper liners in mini-muffin pans. Fill each cup ¾ full of mixture. Freeze for 30 minutes or until set. Remove from freezer and store in airtight container in refrigerator.

JUDITH MILLER, Fredericktown, Ohio

Chocolate Chews

1 cup collagen
¼ cup cocoa or carob powder
2 pinches salt
1 to 2 pinches stevia or honey
   to taste

1 teaspoon vanilla
2 tablespoons butter
1 to 3 tablespoons water

Mix collagen, cocoa, salt, stevia, vanilla, and butter until crumbly. Add 1 tablespoon water. Test crumbs to see if they will stay together. Add more water as needed. Press into small bite-sized pieces. Refrigerate.

MOLLY KINSINGER, Meyersdale, Pennsylvania

Healthy Chocolate Fudge

DAIRY-FREE   EGG-FREE   GLUTEN-FREE

REFINED SUGAR–FREE   VEGAN

1 cup coconut oil
1 cup cocoa powder
1½ cups peanut butter
½ cup maple syrup

½ teaspoon sea salt
2 teaspoons vanilla
2 droppers French
vanilla stevia

Warm coconut oil until melted. Whisk in cocoa. Add peanut butter, maple syrup, salt, vanilla, and stevia. Pat into 8x8-inch pan. Chill. Cut and store in refrigerator.

LINDA MILLER, Gallipolis, Ohio

HOMEMADE PEANUT BUTTER CUPS

🥛 DAIRY-FREE 🌾 GLUTEN-FREE 🥚 EGG-FREE
🚫 LOW-CARB 📦 REFINED SUGAR-FREE

⅓ cup unsweetened cocoa powder
⅓ cup coconut oil, melted

⅓ cup maple syrup
Natural peanut butter

Use blender to blend cocoa powder, coconut oil, and maple syrup until creamy, or whisk well by hand. Put paper liners on cookie sheet. Drop 1 teaspoon of chocolate mixture into each cup. Lift and drop cookie sheet to help chocolate settle. Next, place 1 teaspoon of peanut butter on top of chocolate. Add 1 teaspoon chocolate on top of peanut butter. Again, lift and drop cookie sheet to help chocolate flatten. Place in freezer for at least 20 minutes to allow chocolate to harden. Store in refrigerator or freezer.

LORETTA BRUBAKER, Farmington, Missouri

Bean Fudge

3½ cups cooked navy or black beans, with juice if desired
½ cup coconut oil, melted
¾ cup cocoa powder
½ to ¾ cup maple syrup or agave

½ teaspoon vanilla
⅛ teaspoon salt (use more if beans are unsalted)
½ to ¾ cup crunchy or creamy peanut butter

Blend or use potato masher to mash cooked beans until very smooth. Add remaining ingredients and mix well. Press firmly into 8x8-inch pan. Chill.

Freda Fisher, Leola, Pennsylvania

Coffee Bites

1½ cups peanut butter
½ cup honey
2 cups oatmeal

¼ cup ground coffee
¼ cup chia seeds
¾ cup dark chocolate chips

Combine all ingredients and shape into balls. Refrigerate or freeze.

Freda Fisher, Leola, Pennsylvania

SUGAR-FREE CANDY

DAIRY-FREE **EGG-FREE** **GLUTEN-FREE** **LOW-CARB** **SUGAR-FREE** **VEGAN**

⅔ cup coconut oil
¼ cup xylitol
¼ cup cocoa powder
¼ teaspoon vanilla

1 cup toasted pecans
1 cup toasted shredded
coconut

In saucepan, melt coconut oil and xylitol. Add cocoa and vanilla. Stir in pecans and coconut. Drop by spoonfuls onto waxed paper to cool.

LYDIA MILLER, Loudonville, Ohio

YOGURT STICKS

EGG-FREE **GLUTEN-FREE** **REFINED SUGAR-FREE** **NUT-FREE**

1 cup fruit juice
Dash vanilla

½ cup plain yogurt

Mix all ingredients. Pour into 6 molds and freeze until solid.

MARTHA BEECHY, Butler, Ohio

Miscellaneous Things

*Dear friend, I pray that you may enjoy good
health and that all may go well with you,
even as your soul is getting along well.*

3 John 2

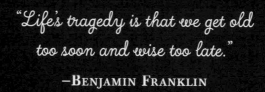

"Life's tragedy is that we get old too soon and wise too late."

—BENJAMIN FRANKLIN

SUBSTITUTES FOR SUGAR

SWEETENER	RATIO TO USE PER 1 CUP SUGAR	DECREASE	ADD	OVEN TEMPERATURE
HONEY	⅔ to ¾ cup	liquid by ¼ cup	¼ tsp. baking soda	decrease 25 degrees
MAPLE SYRUP	⅔ to ¾ cup	liquid by 3 Tbs.	¼ tsp. baking soda	decrease 25 degrees
SUCANAT*	cup for cup	none	none	keep same
STEVIA	1 tsp. liquid or powder	none	add ⅓ bulk	keep same

Sucanat = sucre de canne naturel (natural cane sugar)

Sucanat is a minimally processed, dehydrated cane sugar with the minerals and nutrients still intact. It does not change the texture of cookie dough. It can be used instead of brown sugar. It also comes under the name Rapadura.

MARY MILLER, Junction City, Ohio

GLUTEN-FREE FLOUR MIX

DAIRY-FREE · EGG-FREE · GLUTEN-FREE · NUT-FREE · SUGAR-FREE · VEGAN

2 parts brown rice flour   **1 part tapioca starch**

Mix well and store in airtight container.

LAURA MILLER, Fredericktown, Ohio

Sweet Mix

8 cups erythritol
4 cups birch xylitol

2 tablespoons stevia

In gallon jar or glass container, combine all ingredients well. Make sure there are no clumps of any sweetener. Store in airtight container.

For the most part, this sweetener measures like store-bought Truvia.

⅓ to ½ cup Sweet Mix = 1 cup sugar

If your family tolerates xylitol well, you can use more xylitol than erythritol or equal amounts of both.

Always start with less sweetener than a recipe calls for and gradually add more until the taste is right. This has a pleasant "sugar sweet" taste. Taste will improve, though, after baking and cooling.

Esther Borntrager, Clark, Missouri

Mrs. Miriam Raber, Flat Rock, Illinois

Powdered Sugar Replacement

2 cups nonfat dry
milk powder
2 cups cornstarch

1 cup stevia blend,
Splenda, or xylitol

Combine all ingredients in food processor or blender. Use in place of powdered sugar in most recipes.

Mrs. Albert (Ruth) Yoder, Stanwood, Michigan

Tapioca Starch Substitution

If your recipe calls for tapioca starch (aka tapioca flour) for thickening, you can use 1 tablespoon arrowroot, cornstarch, or flour for every 1½ teaspoons tapioca starch called for (1 tablespoon tapioca starch = 2 tablespoons arrowroot).

Is Spelt Flour Gluten-Free?

Spelt is part of the wheat family, so spelt flour does contain gluten. Some people with a wheat allergy or gluten sensitivity do say that flour made from spelt grain is easier to digest and does not send them into flares.

Is Oatmeal Gluten-Free?

Oatmeal is naturally gluten-free, but most often it is transported and stored in the same equipment as wheat and processed in the same plants. If you are truly gluten sensitive or have celiac disease, look for a brand that is certified "gluten-free."

GLUTEN-FREE COOKIE FLOUR MIX

2 cups white rice flour
1 cup tapioca starch
1½ cups oat flour
¼ cup potato starch or
   potato flour
¼ cup coconut flour

Combine all ingredients. Store in airtight container.

JULIA TROYER, Fredericksburg, Ohio

CAROL'S GLUTEN-FREE SORGHUM FLOUR BLEND

1½ cups sorghum flour
1 cup tapioca flour
1½ cups potato starch or cornstarch
½ cup almond flour or bean flour

Mix well and store in airtight container.

SUSIE E. KINSINGER, Fredericktown, Ohio

Natural Food Colorings

Blue: Boil ½ cup water and ½ cup blueberries for 5 minutes. Strain and store in jar in refrigerator. Makes about 1½ cups.

Brown: Carob powder or syrup can be used to flavor or color frosting.

Green: Boil spinach leaves or alfalfa tea and ½ cup water for 5 minutes. Strain and store in jar in refrigerator. Makes 1 cup.

Orange: Place carrots in blender and grind into small pieces. Add ¼ cup water and blend until smooth. Strain and store in jar in refrigerator. Makes ¼ cup.

Red: Boil 2 cups beets and ¾ cup water for 5 minutes. Strain and store in jar in refrigerator. Use sparingly. Icing will pick up red beet flavor. Makes 1 cup.

Yellow: Add 1 teaspoon saffron to boiling water. Boil for 5 minutes. Strain and store in jar in refrigerator. Makes 1 cup.

Peach: Mix 1 part red and 1 part yellow colorings. Strain and store in jar in refrigerator.

Note: Colorings may be frozen.

HANNAH BEILER, Peach Bottom, Pennsylvania

Sugar-Free Jam or Jelly

DAIRY-FREE **EGG-FREE** **GLUTEN-FREE** **NUT-FREE**

2 tablespoons lemon juice
2 tablespoons unflavored
   gelatin
2 teaspoons cornstarch

Dash salt
2 cups chopped fruit or juice
Sweetener of choice

Mix lemon juice, gelatin, cornstarch, salt, and fruit in saucepan. Let set 10 minutes until gelatin has softened. Bring to boil over high heat, stirring constantly. Cool for 2 minutes, still stirring. Add sweetener to taste. I recommend using stevia. To preserve for future use, pour into 2 jelly jars with 2-piece lids. Process in boiling water bath for 10 minutes. Refrigerate after opening. Yields 1 pint.

Mrs. Joseph Miller, Navarre, Ohio

Strawberry Jam

14 ounces strawberries, sliced

2 tablespoons cold water

1 teaspoon lemon juice

1 tablespoon powdered sugar-free sweetener

1 teaspoon chia seeds, ground

In saucepan, bring strawberries and water to boil and simmer 15 minutes. Only add lemon juice if you want to store jam longer than 1 week. Mash strawberries and cook for 30 minutes until reduced by half. Add sweetener and chia seeds. Stir. Cool. Pour into jars. Store in refrigerator.

IRENE MAST, Kalona, Iowa

Miracle Freezer Jam

1 cup dried pineapple, diced

2 cups fresh or frozen fruit

Place ingredients in blender. Blend well until smooth. Store jam in freezer. Remove from freezer at least 20 minutes before serving.

MARY KING, Kinzers, Pennsylvania

ANNA MILLER, Loudonville, Ohio

Chocolate Syrup

1 cup maple syrup

½ cup cocoa powder

Combine ingredients. Use to make chocolate milk or to top ice cream.

KATIE GINGERICH, Dalton, Ohio

Almond Milk

DAIRY-FREE EGG-FREE GLUTEN-FREE
REFINED SUGAR–FREE VEGAN

½ cup raw almonds
1 tablespoon maple syrup

2 cups water

Place almonds in blender and grind to fine powder. Add maple syrup and 1 cup water. Blend for 1 to 2 minutes to form smooth cream. With blender running on high, slowly add remaining water. Strain with cheesecloth. Store in glass jar in refrigerator for 4 to 5 days.

RACHEL D. MILLER, Millersburg, Ohio

5-Minute Velveeta Cheese

EGG-FREE GLUTEN-FREE LOW-CARB
NUT-FREE SUGAR-FREE

2 tablespoons unflavored
  gelatin
¾ cup instant dry milk
2 cups boiling water

4 cups freshly shredded
  cheddar cheese
1 teaspoon salt

In blender, pulse together gelatin and dry milk. Add boiling water; pulse (be careful if your blender isn't glass, and be sure to vent steam). Add cheese and salt; pulse until smooth. Pour into loaf pan lined with plastic wrap. Cover and refrigerate until solid.

KATIE PETERSHEIM, Mifflin, Pennsylvania

ROSE HIP SYRUP

Rose hip syrup is not difficult to make, and like elderberry syrup, it tastes good and is good for you, as it is full of vitamin C.

In fall, just before or after frost, gather a large amount of rose hips. *Rose hip*s are the round portion of the rose flower just below the petals. Remove blossom end, stems, and any imperfections. Wash well under warm running water. Break down rose hips in food processor or grinder. Put rose hips in large pot and cover with water about an inch over contents. Bring to boil and boil gently for 15 minutes.

Remove from heat and let cool so rose hips are safe to handle. Pour into jelly bag or cheesecloth and let drain overnight. Squeeze bag to remove all juice. You will need to strain twice to remove seeds and particles that would be unpleasant if left in.

Reheat juice until boiling and add enough raw sugar to saturate juice—1 cup sugar to 1 cup juice. Or, if you'd rather, use ½ cup honey to 1 cup juice. Boil gently and stir constantly for 5 to 10 minutes. The juice should reduce and thicken some.

Tasty on pancakes.

SALOMA YODER, Mercer, Missouri

RAW BRICK CHEESE

3 gallons milk
⅛ teaspoon culture
½ teaspoon rennet

¼ cup cool water
2 to 3 tablespoons salt

In 12-quart kettle, heat milk to 98 degrees. Add culture. Stir well. Let set 10 minutes. Dilute rennet in water; add to milk. Mix well. Let set 45 minutes. Reheat to 98 degrees, stirring constantly. Let set 25 minutes. Drain curds for 10 minutes. Add salt. Put in press and press overnight. Air dry for 12 to 24 hours. Best if aged at least 2 weeks.

Note: This is "raw" cheese with all the beneficial bacteria still alive because the milk is not heated over 100 degrees.

MRS. BENUEL BLANK, Delta, Pennsylvania

COTTAGE CHEESE

1 gallon milk
¾ cup vinegar

1½ cups cream
Salt

Heat 1 gallon milk to 190 degrees. Add vinegar, stir, and let set 1 hour. Drain and add cream and salt to your taste.

CEVILLA A. GINGERICH, Dundee, Ohio

DAIRY-FREE YOGURT

DAIRY-FREE · **EGG-FREE** · **GLUTEN-FREE**
LOW-CARB · **SUGAR-FREE**

1 gallon almond or coconut
  milk
½ cup almond or coconut
  yogurt for starter
⅔ cup Sweet Mix or
  1 tablespoon liquid stevia

4 teaspoons vanilla
2 heaping tablespoons
  gelatin
⅔ cup water
Contents of 1 probiotic
  capsule (optional)

Heat milk to 150 degrees. Cool to 110 degrees. Add yogurt, sweetener, and vanilla. Dissolve gelatin in water. Add to milk and stir to further dissolve. Add probiotic if desired. Put 100-degree water in well-insulated cooler and set the pot of milk in it for 8 to 12 hours, or use a slow cooker on "keep warm" setting.

SALOMA YODER, Mercer, Missouri

HOMEMADE YOGURT

EGG-FREE · **GLUTEN-FREE** · **REFINED SUGAR-FREE** · **NUT-FREE**

3 heaping teaspoons
  unflavored gelatin
2 quarts milk
½ cup cold water

6 tablespoons yogurt starter
⅓ cup honey or maple syrup
  (optional)

Dissolve gelatin in water. Heat milk to 180 degrees. Add gelatin. Cool milk to 115 degrees. Add starter and sweetener and beat to mix. Keep at 100 to 110 degrees for 4 to 6 hours or overnight. Beat in flavor of choice. (I use raspberry gelatin or orange drink mix.) Put in containers and refrigerate.

CEVILLA SWARTZENTRUBER, Franklinville, New York

Salad Dressing

GLUTEN-FREE · **LOW-CARB** · **NUT-FREE** · **SUGAR-FREE**

½ cup sugar-free ketchup
½ cup sugar-free mayonnaise
¼ cup vinegar
¼ cup milk
Mustard to taste

½ teaspoon oregano
½ teaspoon parsley
¼ teaspoon chili powder
¼ teaspoon turmeric
¼ teaspoon garlic powder

Combine all ingredients and pour over lettuce salad.

JUDY ZIMMERMAN, East Earl, Pennsylvania

Dairy-Free Ranch Dressing

1 quart mayonnaise
2 teaspoons garlic powder
2 teaspoons onion powder
1 teaspoon dill weed
4 tablespoons parsley

4 tablespoons nutritional yeast
1 teaspoon pepper
½ teaspoon pink or sea salt
Water or almond milk

Mix all ingredients except water or almond milk. Add enough water or almond milk to reach desired consistency for dressing or dip.

Maryann Stauffer, Homer City, Pennsylvania

Italian Dressing

1 cup oil
⅓ cup vinegar
2 tablespoons lemon juice
1 teaspoon garlic salt
1 teaspoon sweetener of your choice

½ teaspoon dry mustard
½ teaspoon oregano
¼ teaspoon basil
¼ teaspoon thyme

Mix all ingredients well and serve. Excellent for marinating chicken and pork chops.

Mable Yoder, Mount Vernon, Ohio

"CHICK-FIL-A" SAUCE

DAIRY-FREE · GLUTEN-FREE · LOW-CARB · NUT-FREE · REFINED SUGAR–FREE

½ cup mayonnaise
2 teaspoons mustard
1 teaspoon lemon juice

2 tablespoons honey
1 tablespoon smoky barbecue sauce

Mix well. Serve with any kind of meat.

Mrs. Ray Hershberger, Scottsville, Michigan

POULTRY SEASONING

DAIRY-FREE · EGG-FREE · GLUTEN-FREE · LOW-CARB · NUT-FREE · SUGAR-FREE · VEGAN

2 tablespoons ground sage
1 tablespoon ground rosemary

1 tablespoon ground thyme

Mix ingredients well and store in airtight container. This is a great alternative to commercial packets that contain MSG.

Susanna Mast, Kalona, Iowa

SEASONED SALT

DAIRY-FREE · EGG-FREE · GLUTEN-FREE · LOW-CARB · NUT-FREE · SUGAR-FREE · VEGAN

1 cup salt
2 tablespoons onion powder
1 tablespoon celery salt
1 teaspoon garlic powder

2 teaspoons paprika
1 teaspoon chili powder
1 teaspoon dried parsley flakes, ground

Combine all ingredients. Store in shaker or jar with lid.

Esther Martin, Fleetwood, Pennsylvania

Homemade Mayonnaise

2 eggs
1 teaspoon salt
2 tablespoons raw sugar
2 tablespoons vinegar

Juice of ½ lemon
1 cup light olive oil
1¼ cups safflower oil

Put eggs in blender and blend well. Add salt, sugar, vinegar, and lemon juice. Blend. Slowly drizzle in both oils until the right consistency is reached.

Using light-tasting oils is important.

KATIE PETERSHEIM, Mifflin, Pennsylvania

TACO SEASONING MIX

🍶 DAIRY-FREE 🥚 EGG-FREE 🌾 GLUTEN-FREE 🥜 NUT-FREE 🥕 VEGAN

3 tablespoons chili powder
1 tablespoon garlic powder
1 tablespoon paprika
1 tablespoon oregano

2 teaspoons salt
2 tablespoons onion powder
1 tablespoon cumin
1 tablespoon sugar

Combine all ingredients and store in freezer. Use 3 tablespoons mix in place of 1 package taco seasoning.

MARY ELLEN WENGERD, Campbellsville, Kentucky

Gluten-Free Taco Shells

1½ cups cold water
1 cup rice flour
½ cup cornmeal

½ teaspoon salt
1 egg

Combine all ingredients with whisk. Fry ½ cup of batter in hot, oiled pan. Rotate the pan to make a flat circle. These shells roll up nicely and can be used with almost any filling. Yields 10 to 12 shells.

ESTHER MARTIN, Fleetwood, Pennsylvania

White Sauce

2 tablespoons butter
2 tablespoons rice flour

¼ teaspoon salt
1 cup milk

Melt butter in saucepan. Add flour and salt, cooking and stirring until bubbly. Whisk in milk. Cook just until smooth and thickened. Makes slightly over 1 cup. For a thick sauce, increase butter and flour to 3 tablespoons each. For a thin sauce, decrease butter and flour to 1 tablespoon each.

LAURA MILLER, Fredericktown, Ohio

Bar-B-Q Sauce

8 cups tomato juice
2 cups chopped onion
½ cup lemon juice
1½ cups apple cider vinegar
1½ tablespoons
 Worcestershire sauce

6 tablespoons mustard
⅓ cup sea salt
2 tablespoons paprika
1 teaspoon stevia
½ cup chia seeds

Combine all ingredients besides chia seeds in kettle and boil for 20 minutes. Add seeds to thicken sauce.

IDA MAST, Kalona, Iowa

Fermented Pepper Mix

3 gallons sweet peppers, cut
 into strips
2 cans ripe black olives
Sliced baby carrots
2 candy onions, sliced
1 head cauliflower, chopped
 (optional)

2 cups olive oil
5 cups white vinegar
5 cups water
1 cup salt
3 tablespoons chopped garlic
¼ cup Italian seasoning

Combine all ingredients in large nonmetal container and cover. Marinate 24 hours. Store in jars with tight lids. No need to heat or vacuum seal. Refrigerate or store in other cool place. This mix is fermented like sauerkraut, so it is full of probiotics and tastes like an Italian salad. We like it on sandwiches or as a small side in winter.

MRS. KRISTINA BYLER, Crab Orchard, Kentucky

HOMEMADE REMEDIES

Therefore confess your sins to each other and pray for each other so that you may be healed. The prayer of a righteous person is powerful and effective.

JAMES 5:16

> *"Let food be thy medicine and medicine be thy food."*
> —HIPPOCRATES

> *A cheerful heart is good medicine,*
> *but a crushed spirit dries up the bones.*
> PROVERBS 17:22

LAUGH MORE

A hearty laugh gives a workout to your stomach and chest muscles, heart, and lungs. Though your blood pressure and adrenaline go up during laughter, they drop down to normal or below afterward, releasing stress.

MRS. JOSEPH J. SCHWARTZ, Salem, Indiana

SIMPLE UNIVERSAL REMEDY

I've found a little remedy to ease the life we live that costs the least and does the most. It is the word *forgive*.

MRS. DAVID KURTZ, Smicksburg, Pennsylvania

PLEASE NOTE:
Don't take anything you read here as replacement for your doctor's advice or emergency medical attention. All home remedies should only be used with a healthy dose of common sense and caution.

Allergies

Allergies may be helped by consuming locally collected honey in several spoonfuls a day.

MOLLY KINSINGER, Meyersdale, Pennsylvania

Echinacea

2 parts fresh echinacea herb, chopped

1 part fresh echinacea root, chopped

1 part peppermint leaves, chopped

Vodka

Glycerin

Pack herbs in jar. Mix half vodka and half glycerin to cover herbs. Let stand at room temperature for 4 weeks, shaking daily. Strain and bottle. Use as an immune booster.

MRS. JONAS GINGERICH, Dalton, Ohio

Adrenal Cocktail

1 to 2 organic lemons, peeled
1½ cups filtered water
1 teaspoon MCT oil
1 teaspoon protein powder
½ teaspoon vanilla
2 pinches salt
½ teaspoon cinnamon
½ teaspoon turmeric
¼ teaspoon ginger
¼ teaspoon nutmeg
Pinch ground clove
¼ teaspoon stevia
2,000 to 4000 mg vitamin C powder
1 to 2 drops lemon Young Living essential oil
Ice cubes

Peel lemons, leaving as much white pith as possible for nutritional benefit. (If lemon is organic, you can use rind.) Slice lemons in quarters and remove seeds. Place lemon in blender. Add all remaining ingredients except ice. Blend well. Pour mixture into quart jar and fill to top with ice. Put lid on jar and shake before drinking.

KATIE MILLER, Arthur, Illinois

ARTERY CLEANSE

1 quart apple juice
1 quart cranberry-grape
juice

1 cup raw apple cider vinegar

Combine all ingredients. Drink ½ cup on empty stomach every morning.

RUTH HOCHSTETLER, Dundee, Ohio

BLACKBERRY ELECTROLYTE DRINK

1 pint water
1 pint blackberry juice
½ teaspoon salt

1 teaspoon baking soda
3 tablespoons sorghum
molasses or honey

Combine all ingredients and serve warm or cold. We find this refreshing and energizing after a bout of fever or stomach disorders.

K. HERTZLER, West Salisbury, Pennsylvania

NATURAL DETOXING AND ENERGIZING DRINK

12 to 16 ounces warm water
2 tablespoons apple cider
vinegar
2 tablespoons lemon juice
½ to 1 teaspoon ground
ginger

¼ teaspoon cinnamon
Dash cayenne pepper
1 teaspoon raw honey

Combine all ingredients and drink warm or cold. If you are looking for an easy way to cleanse your body and boost your energy, have this drink once a day before breakfast or lunch. For more intense detoxification, drink it 3 times per day 20 minutes before meals for 2 weeks.

IVA YODER, Goshen, Indiana

Elderberry Juice

Gather elderberries in summer, wash, and remove most stems. Put in kettle and cover with equal quantity of water. Bring to boil and simmer 5 minutes. Strain. Pour into jars and process in boiling water bath for 10 minutes. Add honey to serve as a good winter drink. When a child is sick, I put this in a bottle for them to slowly sip. Does wonders.

CEVILLA SWARTZENTRUBER, Franklinville, New York

Eldermint Cough Syrup

2 cups fresh elderberry
   blossoms
2 cups fresh peppermint
   leaves

2 cups glycerin
2 cups distilled water or
   boiled water

Put all ingredients in glass jar and let sit for 4 to 6 weeks. Shake daily. Strain and bottle. Take 1 tablespoon for cough.

WILLIAM AND REBECCA TROYER, Navarre, Ohio

Elderberry Fire Water

½ cup boiling water
1 teaspoon salt
½ to 1 teaspoon cayenne

¼ cup vinegar
¼ cup homemade elderberry
   syrup or Sambucol

Combine all ingredients. Take by teaspoon to ward off colds.

FREIDA FISHER, Sprakers, New York

FIRE WATER

¾ to 1 teaspoon cayenne
   pepper
1 teaspoon salt

½ cup boiling water
½ cup apple cider vinegar

At the first sign of a sniffle or cold, combine all ingredients and take 1 tablespoon every 15 minutes for 1 hour. Then cut back to 1 tablespoon an hour until entire cup has been consumed.

LINDA MILLER, Spartansburg, Pennsylvania

MARTHA MILLER, Decatur, Indiana

REBECCA E. STUTZMAN, Gilman, Wisconsin

GINGER TEA

1 tablespoon freshly grated
   ginger
1 slice lemon

1 teaspoon honey
8 ounces boiling water

Steep ginger, lemon, and honey in water for several minutes. Strain and drink. This is a great immune booster and flu fighter.

EMMA MILLER, Baltic, Ohio

LEMON TEA

Squeezing a lemon wedge into your tea turns your drink into a powerful superfood. Lemon increases the level of available antioxidants in the tea. Antioxidants found in white, green, and black tea are more powerful than vitamins C and E in terms of stopping cell damage. And they lower cholesterol levels.

ESTHER MARTIN, Fleetwood, Pennsylvania

THYME TEA

Add 1 teaspoon dried thyme to 1 cup boiling water. Cover and let steep for 20 to 30 minutes. Strain and drink. Thyme heals upper respiratory infections like bronchitis and whooping cough. Thyme is a powerful antiseptic.

MRS. MARTHA BYLER, Atlantic, Pennsylvania

FATIGUE REMEDY

Mix 1 tablespoon apple cider vinegar and 1 tablespoon honey in glass of water. Take upon rising in the morning and before every meal. This drink is good for aches and pains and many other things.

EMMA A. HERSHBERGER, Apple Creek, Ohio

MRS. DAVID KURTZ, Smicksburg, Pennsylvania

GOOD HEALTH REMEDY

Add 1 teaspoon honey and 1 teaspoon apple cider vinegar to a cup of hot tea with lemon. Drink first thing in the morning. Good for sickness prevention, stomach problems, the liver, colitis, and more. May help to get rid of excessive fluid.

EMMA BYLER, New Wilmington, Pennsylvania

MARY MILLER, Junction City, Ohio

LIZZIE H. STUTZMAN, Gilman, Wisconsin

Super Tonic

Hot peppers **Ginger root**
Garlic cloves **Horseradish**
Onions **Apple cider vinegar**

Use equal parts hot pepper, garlic, and onion (for example, a pound each). Use only half as much ginger and horseradish (for example, a half pound each). Grind up all ingredients and cover with apple cider vinegar. Stir every day for 2 weeks. Strain. Bottle and use for colds and coughs. Take by spoonful morning and evening and extra as needed. Can dilute with water for children.

Mrs. Amos B. Eicher, Monroe, Indiana

Hair Loss

Take Bio B-100 (vitamin B complex from a health food store). Also, make tea of sage leaves in 1 pint hot water. Add 1 tablespoon boric acid. Massage tea into scalp daily.

Barbara E. Yoder, Gilman, Wisconsin

Itchy Scalp Remedy

Wash hair with shampoo free of sodium lauryl sulphate, rinse, then cover whole scalp with pure apple cider vinegar and let set for 3 to 5 minutes. Rinse.

Mrs. Kristina Byler, Crab Orchard, Kentucky

Carpal Tunnel Syndrome

Some surgeries may be prevented by taking vitamin B-6 and doing some exercises. Press bottom of chin with both thumbs for several minutes at least once daily. Also, press the tip of your pinkie finger and thumb together, then, resisting, try to pull them apart with your other hand. This builds up wrist muscles.

Barbara E. Yoder, Gilman, Wisconsin

Bee Sting Remedy

Put honey on bee stings. Or make paste with baking soda and water. Coat sting and let dry.

Bethany Martin, Homer City, Pennsylvania

Relief for Bee Stings

Mix equal parts baking soda and vinegar to put on sting. Works very well.

Emma Byler, New Wilmington, Pennsylvania

Insect Bite Remedy

For insect bite, apply slice of raw onion on area.

Emma Byler, New Wilmington, Pennsylvania

Mosquito Bite Remedy

Moisten bar of soap and rub on bite. It will relieve itching and act as disinfectant to prevent infection.

Mattie Petersheim, Junction City, Ohio

Earache Remedy #1

Using vapor chest rub or other salve, rub it right in front of the ears and right behind them all the way down the neck. Use firm pressure but not too hard for young ones. Always rub down and not upward. Also rub it beneath the jawbone, starting beneath the ear and working forward to the chin. Do this several times. Good for sore throat as well.

Mrs. Samuel Lee, Plymouth, Illinois

Earache Remedy #2

Chop up onion finely. Put on square cloth such as handkerchief. Bring up corners and twist cloth around onion. Keep twisting and squeezing until you have enough juice to put a few drops in aching ear. It's that simple and really does work. I like to warm the drops a little. You can also put a warm bag of rice over the ear after applying drops.

Martha Troyer, Millersburg, Ohio

Ear Oil

8 cloves garlic, minced fine　　**Olive oil**
2 tablespoons mullein

Place garlic and mullein in double boiler and just cover with olive oil. Keep mixture hot for 2 hours. Do not boil. Strain into glass jar and store in refrigerator. To use, warm and drop two drops into infected ear. Will usually dry up fluid behind eardrum or cure ear infection if used regularly.

Mrs. Kristina Byler, Crab Orchard, Kentucky

Garlic Salve

⅓ cup coconut oil

2 tablespoons olive oil

8 cloves peeled garlic

5 drops lavender oil, optional

In blender, blend all ingredients on high speed. Can be strained to remove garlic pieces. Stores in refrigerator for a long time.

Use on chest and bottom of feet for colds, coughs, respiratory syncytial virus (RSV), and pneumonia. For earaches, place salve on cotton swab and rub around ear.

RUTH HOCHSTETLER, Dundee, Ohio

I like to add several drops of frankincense oil.

LINDA MILLER, Spartansburg, Pennsylvania

REBECCA E. STUTZMAN, Gilman, Wisconsin

Green Salve

⅓ part comfrey leaves
⅓ part calendula flowers
⅓ part plantain
Olive oil

Wax
Vitamin E oil capsules
Chamomile, lavender,
   or tea tree oil

Put comfrey, calendula, and plantain in jar. Cover with olive oil. Seal jar. Place jar in paper bag and set in sun for 2 to 6 weeks. Strain and press herbs to capture every bit of oil. Measure oil. For every ounce of oil, add 1 tablespoon grated wax and 1 capsule vitamin E oil. Add a few drops of chamomile, lavender, or tea tree oil for scent.

This is a mighty all-purpose salve. Very good for diaper rash, cuts, dry hands, and more.

LYDIA RUTH BYER, Newburg, Pennsylvania

Marigold Salve

Heat 4 cups olive oil in iron skillet until you see heat waves. Add as many marigold blossoms as you can easily fit into skillet. Fry until blossoms start to brown. Remove blossoms and strain oil. Add 3 ounces beeswax to oil, stirring as it cools. This is a very useful salve to keep on hand for most any ailment.

LINDA MILLER, Spartansburg, Pennsylvania

Salve for Burns

1 gram alum   2 egg whites
1 cup lard

Mix alum into lard. Add egg whites and mix thoroughly. Very effective for large burns. Spread on cloth and cover burn area. Also good for sunburns. Keep in small containers in freezer to have ready when needed.

MRS. SAMUEL LEE, Plymouth, Illinois

Burn Remedy

If you burn your finger or hand, plunge it into flour. Some people keep some flour in freezer to use on burns.

BETHANY MARTIN, Homer City, Pennsylvania

Painful Burn Tips

- Mix equal parts castor oil and cod liver oil. Soak cotton ball or cloth with mixture and lay on burn. Cotton is said to be better than gauze. Relieves pain quickly.
- Vaseline is said to stop pain in burns almost immediately.
- Dip burned hand in cold fresh skimmed cream or top milk to relieve pain.
- Puncture vitamin E capsule and put pure oil directly on burn or other sore. Heals burn quickly and prevents scars.

LIZZIE H. STUTZMAN, Gilman, Wisconsin

Sunburn Remedy

Put apple cider vinegar on sunburns that have not blistered. Will prevent peeling if applied immediately after exposure.

BETHANY MARTIN, Homer City, Pennsylvania

BARBARA E. YODER, Gilman, Wisconsin

Bleeding Cuts

To stop small cuts from bleeding, dust with cayenne pepper. Works well and will not burn a fresh cut. For a cut that won't stop bleeding, cover it with honey and wrap with a bandage such as strips of white sheets.

BARBARA E. YODER, Gilman, Wisconsin

CUT REMEDY

Use the skin (the layer just inside the shell) of a raw egg to put over cuts to hold them together. Leave it on until it peels off by itself.

EMMA BEILER, Delta, Pennsylvania

DRAWING AGENT

To draw infection from a sore, stir a teaspoon of salt into an egg yolk. Apply to sore and cover with cloth.

LIZZIE H. STUTZMAN, Gilman, Wisconsin

INFECTED AREA REMEDY

Mix charcoal and ground flaxseed with castor oil to form spreadable paste. To pull glass, dirt, or other particle from skin sore, apply mixture to sore area.

My husband had a sore/hurting spot on his shoulder. We put the mixture on it. The skin broke open, and out came pus. It healed up, though he does have a scar. No idea what caused it.

LENA TROYER, Redding, Iowa

SORE REMEDY

Scrape a potato finely and tie pulp over sore. It is said to heal when all other remedies have failed.

LIZZIE H. STUTZMAN, Gilman, Wisconsin

Open Sore Remedy

Set up 2 dishpans. In first pan, place ¼ cup Epsom salt in 1 gallon hot water (120 degrees). In second pan, place ¼ cup Epsom salt in 1 gallon water with ice cubes.

Use 2 white Turkish towels. Soak one in hot water and wrap around sore (generally used on arms or legs) for 3 minutes. Remove and wrap cold water–soaked towel around sore for 2 minutes. Repeat hot soak. Always start and end with hot soak. Do this process morning and evening. Dress sore with B&W (burn and wound) ointment and burdock in between.

Rebecca E. Stutzman, Gilman, Wisconsin

Corn and Sore Remedy

Dip cotton ball in peppermint oil and tape over corn or sore. Leave on 3 to 4 days then soak area in warm water. Repeat as necessary.

Lizzie H. Stutzman, Gilman, Wisconsin

Pinched Fingers and Toes

Wrap pinched area in fresh plantain leaves that you find in the lawn. When I got my finger caught in the washing machine wringer, I put some crushed plantain leaves on my finger, and the throbbing soon stopped.

Lena Troyer, Redding, Iowa

Mouth Sore Remedy

Moisten finger and dip into powdered alum. Place alum on sore. Hold in mouth awhile then spit it out. Sores heal fast with this remedy.

Bethany Martin, Homer City, Pennsylvania

TOOTHACHE REMEDY #1

Beat together 1 egg white and 1 teaspoon black pepper. Rub on outside of cheek over painful area.

EMMA A. HERSHBERGER, Apple Creek, Ohio

TOOTHACHE REMEDY #2

To stop toothache, soak cotton in ammonia and apply to aching tooth.

MATTIE PETERSHEIM, Junction City, Ohio

Cold Remedy

Dice medium onion into pint jar. Add 1 teaspoon brown sugar. Let stand for 1 hour before using. Give 2 to 3 teaspoonfuls to children every hour.

Emma Byler, New Wilmington, Pennsylvania

Sore Throat Remedy

Mix vinegar with strong dash of salt and red or black pepper. Gargle with it often.

Barbara E. Yoder, Gilman, Wisconsin

Cold and Sore Throat Remedy

1 cup boiling water
1½ teaspoons salt
2 teaspoons red pepper

2 tablespoons honey
1 cup apple cider vinegar

Pour boiling water into quart jar or kettle with lid. Add salt, red pepper, and honey. Cover with lid and let cool. Shake or stir mixture well several times. Add vinegar. Always make sure to shake or stir well before using. Take 1 teaspoonful as often as you wish.

Mrs. Samuel Lee, Plymouth, Illinois

Sore Throat Wrap

Soak a standard pillowcase in cold water. Wring out and wrap around neck. Cover cold wrap with dry flannel pillowcase. Go to bed and rest. The coldness draws out the pain.

Emma Miller, Baltic, Ohio

Chest Cold Remedy

2 teaspoons red pepper
2 teaspoons dry mustard
2 teaspoons baking soda

2 tablespoons flour
½ cup lard

Combine all ingredients. Put some in a cloth, fold, and pin on night clothes over the chest. Leave overnight.

REBECCA E. STUTZMAN, Gilman, Wisconsin

Cold or Pneumonia Remedy

In saucepan, heat 2 tablespoons lard, 2 tablespoons kerosene, and 2 tablespoons turpentine until fat melts and is hot to touch. Rub warm mixture on back and chest. Soak small cloth in mixture and put on chest. Cover with warm flannel.

MATTIE PETERSHEIM, Junction City, Ohio

Cough Poultice

1 teaspoon cinnamon
1 teaspoon allspice
1 teaspoon nutmeg

½ teaspoon ginger
1 teaspoon dry mustard
Lard

Mix spices and work in enough lard to make a paste. Spread on throat and or chest.

MARY STUTZMAN, West Salem, Ohio

Chest Rub

Mix equal parts household ammonia, turpentine, and castor oil. Rub on chest and back. Cover with warm cloth. This will not blister, so you can put it on heavily, and it can be used on babies and children. In severe cases, repeat every 2 to 3 hours. Never fails me for bronchitis, chest tightness, or pneumonia.

EMMA A. HERSHBERGER, Apple Creek, Ohio

Grandma's Lung Fever Salve

3 pounds lard
2 packages Red Man tobacco
1 pound raisins

4 medium onions, chopped
2 teaspoons camphor

Melt lard. Add tobacco, raisins, and onions. Boil slowly at least 30 minutes. Add camphor. When melted, strain and put into jars. When needed, rub on chest and back. Cover with thick warm cloth. Can be used for pneumonia. Safe on babies.

MRS. SAMUEL LEE, Plymouth, Illinois

ONION POULTICE

Chop or thinly slice a few onions. Put in saucepan with 2 or 3 tablespoons lard and fry until slightly browned. Remove from heat and add 1 or 2 tablespoons apple cider vinegar and enough cornmeal to make a poultice. Don't make too dry. Put between 2 old rags and cover or fold up edges. Put it on chest overnight or use immediately if needed. This is a remedy to try before going to the doctor for chest colds or coughs. If one application doesn't work, try again.

EMMA BEILER, Delta, Pennsylvania

PNEUMONIA POULTICE

Shave flakes off bar of homemade soap. Add to hot water to make paste. Stir in bran or whole wheat flour to thicken it. (Bran like that fed to livestock works.) Make a poultice. Put on against chest as hot as you can stand. We have used it for all ages, from babies to the elderly.

MARY STUTZMAN, West Salem, Ohio

VIRUS REMEDY

Drop diluted oregano essential oil in carrier oil, spread along spine, and rub in well.

KATHRYN TROYER, Rutherford, Tennessee

FEVER REMEDY

For fever, beat egg white until foamy and add a little sugar and hot water. Drink it, and you will be surprised at how soon the fever will be gone.

MRS. CARLISLE SCHMIDT, Carlisle, Kentucky

COUGH AND RUNNY NOSE REMEDY

Mix equal amounts of dried chamomile leaves and dried oregano. Add 1 teaspoon of dried mixture to 1 cup boiling water. Let steep 5 minutes, strain, and drink.

KATHRYN TROYER, Rutherford, Tennessee

COUGH REMEDY TEA

1 part thyme leaves
1 part plantain leaves
1 part peppermint leaves

Equal parts vodka and glycerin

Mix herbs and fill a glass jar half full with them. Mix vodka and glycerin. Fill jar with liquid mixture. Let sit for 6 weeks and shake daily. Strain and bottle.

TEA:

Use ½ teaspoon herb tincture per cup of hot water. Sip a cup several times a day. If given promptly and often, coughs (whooping, bronchial, asthma, and pneumonia) will usually not stand a chance.

WILLIAM AND REBECCA TROYER, Navarre, Ohio

SOOTHING COUGH SYRUP

3 cups water
3 tablespoons honey

3 large cloves garlic
1 tablespoon fenugreek seed

Put all in saucepan and boil until it reduces down to ½ cup syrup. May take 1 teaspoonful as needed.

K. HERTZLER, West Salisbury, Pennsylvania

Whooping Cough Remedy

Put 3 or 4 chestnut leaves in 2 cups boiling water. Steep several minutes. Strain and sweeten with honey. Let children drink some 5 or 6 times a day.

Mattie Petersheim, Junction City, Ohio

Mary H. Stutzman, Gilman, Wisconsin

Whooping Cough Syrup

1 lemon, thinly sliced
1 cup flaxseed

1 quart water
2 ounces honey

In saucepan, simmer lemon, flaxseed, and water for 4 hours. Do not boil. You may need to add more water when cool. Strain while hot. Add honey. Measure; if less than 2 cups, add water. Give 1 tablespoon every 4 hours or as needed.

Emma Beiler, Delta, Pennsylvania

This works well to dispel mucous. Take some after every coughing spell up to a cup a day. Great for whooping cough or any other lingering cough.

Lydia Ruth Byer, Newburg, Pennsylvania

Emma A. Hershberger, Apple Creek, Ohio

This remedy has never been known to fail me. Effective for curing cough in children in 4 to 5 days if given before first whoops begin.

Rosina Schwartz, Salem, Indiana

Mary H. Stutzman, Gilman, Wisconsin

Fainting (Dizzy Spells)

A drink of vinegar is a sure cure for fainting.

Barbara Hershberger, Fredericksburg, Ohio

Barbara E. Yoder, Gilman, Wisconsin

Dehydration Remedy

Rub young children with warm olive oil on back and belly until skin doesn't absorb any more. Supposedly this feeds them through the skin, preventing dehydration.

SALOMA YODER, Mercer, Missouri

Homemade Electrolyte Drink

1 pint water
Juice from 1 whole lemon or
orange

½ teaspoon baking soda
2 tablespoons sugar
Pinch salt

Stir all ingredients until sugar dissolves. This drink will help keep child or adult from dehydrating when they cannot keep anything down. Give child 1 teaspoon every 15 minutes. If you give more, the child will throw it up. A teaspoon is enough only to wet the tongue and won't cause stomach upset.

KATHRYN TROYER, Rutherford, Tennessee

Remedy for Lengthy Stomach Bug

28 ounces Gatorade
1 teaspoon sugar

½ teaspoon salt

Fill an empty 28-ounce Gatorade bottle with half water and half Gatorade. Add sugar and salt. Cap the bottle and shake until sugar and salt dissolve.

This recipe was given to us by a doctor when one of our boys had flu and diarrhea for 2 weeks. It is okay to give to small children so they don't dehydrate when sick.

EMMA A. HERSHBERGER, Apple Creek, Ohio

Colitis or Stomach Remedy

Carefully take a cupful of red-hot charcoal from burned wood and put into 2 cups boiling water. Strain. Sip liquid throughout the day. May be repeated 2 to 3 days later.

MATTIE PETERSHEIM, Junction City, Ohio

Red Beet Tonic

When you are canning beets, use plenty of water as you cook beets. Strain off water.

ADD:

   2 gallons water
   14½ pounds sugar
   4 slices whole wheat bread

   4 cakes or tablespoons dry
   yeast

Put beet water and water in large crock or pail. Stir in sugar. Toast bread and spread 1 tablespoon yeast on each slice. Flip yeast-side down on top of beet water. Cover container with white 100 percent cotton cloth. Let stand for 3 weeks. Strain and bottle liquid.

Use 1 tablespoon tonic 2 to 3 times a day for blood tonic or purifier. We also like to use it at start of stomach flu or upset.

Recipe may be cut in half for a smaller batch.

Tonic will keep for more than a year.

LYDIA HERSHBERGER, Dalton, Ohio
LIZZIE H. STUTZMAN, Gilman, Wisconsin

LACTOSE ISSUES?

Can't tolerate cow's milk? Set fresh milk in ice water for 12 hours, then skim off cream. Refrigerate cream for another 12 hours and separate cream again. Then take cream that was skimmed and add water to desired consistency. This can often be used for babies too. Removing whey makes milk more digestible.

K. HERTZLER, West Salisbury, Pennsylvania

HOMEMADE LAXATIVE

1 pint hot water
2 tablespoons Epsom salt

½ tablespoon cream of tartar

Combine and drink ½ cup or more first thing in the morning. To be used only occasionally as the need arises.

MARY STUTZMAN, West Salem, Ohio

Preventative

To prevent kidney or bladder infections, take a probiotic regularly.

MRS. DAVID KURTZ, Smicksburg, Pennsylvania

Blood Tonic

6 lemons
6 oranges
6 grapefruit

4 tablespoons Epsom salt
1 quart boiling water

Grind up lemons, oranges, and grapefruit, including rinds. Sprinkle ground citrus with Epsom salt. Cover with boiling water. Let stand overnight. Next morning, strain through cloth bag and press out juice. Take 1 tablespoon 3 times a day. Keep in cool place as it will spoil. Can reduce size of batch.

MARY H. STUTZMAN, Gilman, Wisconsin

Cancer Tonic

1 quart water
1 cup bloodroot
2 cups clover blossoms

1 tablespoon ginger
1 pint quality whiskey

Bring water to boil and add bloodroot, clover blossoms, and ginger. Boil down to 1 pint. Strain. Add liquid to whiskey. Take a teaspoonful 3 times a day.

MARY H. STUTZMAN, Gilman, Wisconsin

Gallstone Flush

Eat a light breakfast (example: 1 piece of dry toast and 1 cup tea). Drink 1 gallon apple juice from morning until 3 p.m. Stop drinking at 3 p.m. even if juice still remains. Consume nothing else before bedtime. Squeeze lemons to make ½ cup fresh juice. Add ½ cup olive oil in pint jar. Put on lid and shake until thoroughly mixed. Drink all at once just before retiring to bed. Lie on your right side as long as comfortable.

ELAM AND SARAH BEILER, Doylesburg, Pennsylvania

Pneumonia or Flu Foot Soak

1 to 2 tablespoons
dry mustard

1 to 2 teaspoons ginger

1 to 2 teaspoons cayenne
pepper

Mix all in pail of hot water and soak feet for 15 to 20 minutes.

Mrs. Martha Byler, Atlantic, Pennsylvania

Hot Bath Soak

When the day has been long and trying and you are overtired, wonderful relief will result from a hot bath. Add 1 cup Epsom salt and 2 tablespoons dry mustard. Your aching muscles will feel renewed the next morning.

Add bicarbonate of soda to the bathwater to kill perspiration odor.

Lizzie H. Stutzman, Gilman, Wisconsin

Dry Skin Soak

1 cup baking soda

2 cups Epsom salt

1 drop peppermint
essential oil

2 drops bergamot or
orange essential oil

Add all ingredients to bathtub full of hot water. Soak and relax for 20 to 30 minutes.

Emma Miller, Baltic, Ohio

Vanilla-Lavender Bath Salts

2 cups Epsom salt
½ cup baking soda
¼ cup sea salt, optional
10 drops lavender
   essential oil

10 drops vanilla essential
   oil or 1 teaspoon vanilla
   extract
A few drops food coloring,
   optional

Place all ingredients in mixing bowl and mix until well blended. Store in airtight container for up to 6 months. When ready to use, pour ¼ cup bath salts into warm bathwater. Relax and enjoy the calming scents.

Try replacing lavender and vanilla essential oils with oil blends of your choice.

Benefits of salt baths include stress relief, reduced muscle and joint aches, improved circulation, headache relief, improved sleep, improved skin hydration, and help for acne, eczema, or other skin problems.

ADA J. MAST, Kalona, Iowa

Onion Germ Trap

I always have a dish of chopped onions sitting out in the living room and kitchen during winter. If there is some sickness going around, I put out more dishes. Seems to help.

RUTH MILLER, Millersburg, Ohio
CEVILLA SWARTZENTRUBER, Franklinville, New York

Natural Bleach

12 cups water
1 cup peroxide

¼ cup lemon juice

Combine all ingredients and store in vinegar jug. Keep tightly closed. Spray on stains and let set 10 minutes before washing. It may discolor colored clothing. Also useful for cleaning countertops. Cleaning power will decline after a month.

RACHEL D. MILLER, Millersburg, Ohio

Hand Sanitizer

¾ cup rubbing alcohol
¼ cup aloe vera gel

10 drops lavender oil
or lemon oil

Mix all ingredients and put in soap dispenser clearly marked for hand sanitizer.

ESTHER L. MILLER, Fredericktown, Ohio

FOAMING HAND SOAP

⅔ cup unscented liquid
   Castile soap
1⅓ cups distilled water

⅛ teaspoon essential
   oil of choice

Pour ingredients into empty foaming soap dispenser. Shake well. We like to use 3 Thieves essential oil in this.

LINDA BURKHOLDER, Fresno, Ohio

BASIC HAND SOAP

3 cups olive oil
3 cups coconut oil
2½ pounds lard or tallow
1 quart warm water
12½ ounces lye

4 ounces essential oil
   of choice
Chopped herb (like
   spearmint), optional

In stockpot, heat olive oil, coconut oil, and lard to melt. Cool to 90 to 96 degrees. In bowl, slowly mix warm water with lye. Cool to 86 to 90 degrees. Mix lye into oils and stir with a straight spoon for a few minutes. Then stir occasionally until it traces (thickens enough that you could write your name on it). Add essential oil and optional herb. Mix well and pour into molds or trays. Cut while still a little soft. Let set in molds or trays for 2 days then separate into bars and let air dry for 2 to 4 weeks.

MRS. JONAS GINGERICH, Dalton, Ohio

All-Purpose Vinegar Cleaner

Heat 3 cups apple cider vinegar. Add 1 cup Dawn dish detergent. Let cool and pour into spray bottle. Use to clean sinks, showers, and more. Pour some in toilet to clean.

Mrs. Robert (Shirley) Schlabach, Crofton, Kentucky

Safe Insect Spray for Gardens

1 teaspoon red pepper
1 teaspoon garlic salt

1 teaspoon onion salt
1 pint hot water

Mix all ingredients and let stand 2 days. Strain. Put in gallon sprayer and fill with water.

Jerry and Mary Girod, Carlisle, Kentucky

Organic Weed Killer

1 gallon white vinegar
3 cups salt

½ bottle dish washing soap

Heat vinegar and dissolve salt in it, stirring well. Add soap and mix well. Put on weeds with a sprinkler can. Use generously.

Marie D. Hershberger, Laurelville, Ohio

THE BEST COOKS

I used to think that the really good cooks
were the ones who threw away all of the books
and whipped up their dishes and specialties hot,
with a stir of the spoon in a large boiling pot.

The pies were the richest, the dumplings the thickest,
and the comments from the guests were the loudest and quickest.
The food tasted good with each bite they gulped down.
And the family proclaimed her the best cook in town.

But nowadays I've read what the books have to say:
it's the pies and the dumplings they should throw away,
and the rest of the starches and pastries they eat,
all the gooey and sticky cakes and candy so sweet.

Nutritionally speaking, the best cooks around
serve you salads and fruits that are rich from the ground.
Foods whole and natural prepared the right way
so their life-giving strength will be left to stay.

LENA YODER, McClure, Pennsylvania

Index of Contributors

Index of Recipes by Section

Desserts

Snacks and Candy

Miscellaneous Things

HOMEMADE REMEDIES

INDEX OF RECIPES BY KEY INGREDIENTS